The Morality of China in Africa

ABOUT THE EDITOR

STEPHEN CHAN OBE is Professor of International Relations at the School of Oriental and African Studies, University of London, where he has twice been Dean. He won the 2010 International Studies Association prize, Eminent Scholar in Global Development. He was a member of the Trilateral Dialogue on China, Africa and the United States. www.stephen-chan.com

The Morality of China in Africa

The Middle Kingdom and the Dark Continent

EDITED BY STEPHEN CHAN

Zed Books

LONDON & NEW YORK

The Morality of China in Africa:
The Middle Kingdom and the Dark Continent was first published in 2013
by Zed Books Ltd, 7 Cynthia Street, London N1 9JF, UK
and Room 400, 175 Fifth Avenue, New York, NY 10010, USA

www.zedbooks.co.uk

Editorial copyright © Stephen Chan 2013
Copyright in this collection © Zed Books 2013

The right of Stephen Chan to be identified as the editor
of this work has been asserted by him in accordance with
the Copyright, Designs and Patents Act, 1988

Designed and typeset in ITC Bodoni Twelve
by illuminati, Grosmont
Index by John Barker
Cover design: www.roguefour.co.uk

A catalogue record for this book is available from the British Library
Library of Congress Cataloging in Publication Data available

ISBN 978 1 78032 567 5 hb
ISBN 978 1 78032 566 8 pb

Contents

Preface

STEPHEN CHAN

The idea for this book first came to me in 2007 in Beijing. I was a member of the Trilateral Dialogue that sought to find a way forward amidst forebodings of a trade war between China and the United States over Africa. Sponsored by the Brenthurst Foundation of South Africa, the membership of the Dialogue was of a very high level. It was not an intergovernmental, or 'Track One', official series of gatherings. But it was not convincingly 'Track Two', or non-governmental, either. I characterized it as 'Track One and a Quarter' as almost every member had instant or swift access to official machinery in his or her home capital, and some were still serving members of governments. On the US side, the members had been cabinet members or deputy and assistant secretaries of state from the Carter through to the Clinton administration, or senior diplomats. Each could justly claim to have critically influenced or changed US policy towards Africa. On the African side, the members included the king of Lesotho, the former prime minister of Angola, former senior diplomats, and serving cabinet ministers. The Chinese side was led by a deputy minister, and at first glance was not of the calibre of the other two. They were characterized as senior scholars who worked on Africa – but each had access to Politburo members, whom they briefed and advised.

The discussions were conducted in South Africa, in China and in the United States. At the Beijing meeting I was struck by two things. The first was the careful arrangement of the conference table, where the Chinese delegation faced the chairman, and two rows of side tables accommodated the Americans and the Africans, who faced each other. Ideally, the Africans should have faced the chair and the two sides competing with each other over Africa should have, like all good adversaries, faced each other. As it was, it was the Chinese who faced directly the arbitrator of proceedings. Planted as an intervening barrier which kept the tables apart was an indoor garden of red flowers.

It was probably inadvertent, but I was both bemused and amused by what I took to be subtle Chinese symbolism. But, then, I suppose the Chinese took my inclusion with the African delegation as some sort of symbol as well. They were too polite to say so but on another visit, in meetings for other purposes with a less accomplished Chinese delegation, they did. I thought therefore that the Chinese sought to lace their work in Africa with symbolism and were perhaps themselves bemused when no one understood them – while they themselves understood symbolism in their own terms.

The second thing that struck me was how poorly prepared the Chinese were at the Trilateral Dialogue meeting. The briefing papers prepared by their academic advisers and supporters were, without exception, appalling. None encompassed what a Western-trained scholar would call research, problematization and interrogation of received wisdom. It was all received wisdom.

It was a parade of academic work to justify Party views of China and Africa.

The Chinese neither understood Africa well, nor did a very good job in projecting what seemed to me a constant underlying but never directly articulated theme, that what China was doing in Africa was moral. When, months later, the Trilateral Dialogue was conducted in Washington DC, it became very clear to me that the Americans felt there was no moral thread at all in the Chinese approach to Africa. In the midst of all of this, the African delegation was well received, listened to with circumspect politeness, assiduously thanked, and I think largely ignored. But it was the African delegation that sought to make some common and moral sense of it all, and its findings are included in this volume,

When the Dialogue was completed I thought about putting this book together. I had two purposes in mind. First, I wanted a collection of essays that proposed a moral underpinning to China's views and actions in Africa. However, I found none. So I decided to write a foundation essay on this topic; it is the first chapter in this volume. However, I am diasporic Chinese. I have perhaps an imperfect, or romantic, or simply wrong view of Chinese morality. So it was important to have less diasporic commentaries on what I wrote. All the other Chinese contributors to this volume, charged with commenting on my paper, were born in mainland China – with the exception of Jerry Liu, who was born in Taiwan. All have Western Ph.D.s and all live outside the mainland as successful Western-based scholars. None is bound to a Party line.

Jerry Liu finds in my writing resonance with his knowledge of Chinese moral culture, but argues that this moral culture is a deliberate usage in the projection of Chinese soft power. Qing Cao cautions that times are changing swiftly, not only for Africa but for China, and pragmatic as opposed to moral goals are increasingly at stake. Lily Ling interrogates deeply my central metaphor of a famous contest for the heart and mind of an 'other', and, like Qing Cao, indicates a deep pragmatism at work; she also makes the sharp point that China could do with some of its so-called moral virtue in Africa back home in China itself. Xiaoming Huang, in an almost abrupt contribution, simply says 'forget China'; it is the world and all global forces and relations that are changing; it could be China in Africa, it could be anyone in Africa; the important thing for Africa is to be itself a force in the global currents that are now raging.

If it could be anyone else in Africa it seemed to me proper to include a final chapter by a distinguished Indian scholar, warning that, if it's to be anyone else, it could well be India in Africa. All this fuss about China – amidst other actors also increasing their investments and their stakes in the continent.

My second purpose was to present an African response. I found there was very little African scholarship devoted to the issue of China–Africa relations as a whole. There is a slowly developing literature on specific case studies. In the end, I approached my colleague on the Trilateral Dialogue, Patrick Mazimhaka. Patrick had been deputy chairman of the Council of the African Union, and, from his experience and thinking in high diplomatic office, would be able to comment broadly and authoritatively. He has done that, and he has also taken a cue from my own personal experience of aspects of the Chinese relationship with Africa. Patrick recounts how, as a very young man, he also had been impressed by Chinese assistance to the project of liberty-by-force-of-arms in Africa. He saw this with his own eyes, as did I, and there is nothing any Western criticism can do to take away this history of armed comradeship. Africa had to struggle, and not many came to help. China did and China never went away. China's first arrival in modern Africa is still remembered by those who saw and felt it.

The volume is therefore, with the exception of Sumit Roy's end piece on India, written entirely by Chinese and Africans. All are outside the circle of 'usual suspects' now regularly rounded up to comment on China and Africa. And all have indeed been able to say something about the moral centrepiece of my essay. I am not pretending the Chinese have not been, or are not now, self-centred, self-seeking, duplicitous, deceitful, opportunistic, even downright wicked in their dealings with Africa. What I am saying is that such statecraft is not the whole story. That story has a subliminal core, a romanticized normativity. It has unnoticed symbolism. It deserves to be banished from our contemplation no more than the Western saturation of all things with democracy, transparency and neoliberalism. The competition for Africa has some philosophical ingredients, if not core. It is for Africa one day, as Patrick Mazimhaka suggests, to answer philosophically as well as economically. I suspect it is already starting to do so.

PART I

The Middle Kingdom
and the Dark Continent

I

The Middle Kingdom and the Dark Continent: an essay on China, Africa and many fault lines

STEPHEN CHAN

In 1980, during the fraught transition of Rhodesia to Zimbabwe, I encountered officers in Mugabe's guerrilla army who ate with chopsticks. They informed me of the range of skills, military as well as culinary, they had learnt from their Chinese instructors.[1] It was a sobering and moving experience for me as a young man who, as an alienated part of the Chinese diaspora, had actively sought to escape Chineseness. I couldn't escape it even in the tensest part of Africa. The struggle between black and white had yellow inputs. I always hated such terms, but my dining companions looked upon me as an unusual representative, but a representative all the same, of a land that had come to their aid. If I lived and worked in Africa, I could not escape China. At that time, the image of China was divided between heroic assistance – in both liberation struggles and developmental efforts – and the romance of pony-tailed Shaolin fighters in the ubiquitous kung fu films. In many African countries, they were

---

1. Stephen Chan, *The Commonwealth Observer Group in Zimbabwe: A Personal Memoir*, Gweru: Mambo Press, 1985.

the only films cinemas could afford to screen. There was a brief moment when being Chinese in Africa, especially if wearing long hair, was a passport to admiration. That is not the case now. This is an essay about the years of Chinese involvement in post-independence Africa, about its romance and philosophy, its achievements and failures; and about outlooks and forebodings. It is about something I never looked upon with academic eyes – so even now I look askance at the academic fashion that is fascinated by the 'new' Chinese penetration of Africa.[2] It is something which intruded upon my peripheral vision over thirty years of involvement with Africa, until it became a monster in my path. It was deposited in my path, more like a pile of elephant dung than a living, complex elephant. Everyone kept asking me questions about Chinese dung in an already dark continent. No one really wanted to understand China and fewer wanted to understand Africa. They just wanted to know about the 'sudden' arrival of a lot of shit in the Western outlook on resource-expropriation from Africa. There is much more to Africa than China – so this is an essay to write China out of my way, to explain China in Africa to my readers, and to render Africa as several complex countries that will – thank you very much – decide their own futures, with or without China.

Elephant dung, by the way, can be turned into very good, odour-free fertilizer, paper products, and parts of paintings by Chris Ofili.

The academic fashion mirrors an international political concern. It was recently a minor panic, especially in the United

---

2. Although there are a small number of excellent, deeply and historically informed works: Ian Taylor, *China and Africa: Engagement and Compromise*, London: Routledge, 2006; Chris Alden, *China in Africa*, London: Zed Books, 2007; Chris Alden, Daniel Large and Richardo Soares De Oliveira, eds, *China Returns to Africa: A Rising Power and a Continent Embrace*, London: Hurst, 2008; Deborah Brautigam, *The Dragon's Gift: The Real Story of China in Africa*, Oxford: Oxford University Press, 2009.

States. Throughout the Cold War, the Americans had been acutely aware of China – but little of this was to do with China in Africa. Henry Kissinger made special efforts to detach the Chinese from any residual sense of Communist identification with the Soviet Union. This was not to court China for the sake of China. It was to neutralize China as a unilateral actor in the global power struggles of the day. It was to allow the United States to contemplate the Soviet Union as the only other actor in a two-actor game. Three-actor games are hard to model, so a Sino–American rapprochement allowed a clean Soviet–American confrontation. China was to be given its own security space in East Asia. It allowed the USA to scale back its involvement in Vietnam, on the understanding that the Chinese would not scale up their involvements outside their own security zone – that is, not intrude upon established Western economic interests and alliances in Taiwan, Japan and Southeast Asian countries outside the Vietnam, Laos and Cambodia triptych.[3]

In the Henry Kissinger years, the USA did not view Africa as a major foreign-policy concern. Provided South Africa, even if under apartheid, remained secure as a provider of raw materials and a guardian of the shipping waters around the Cape of Good Hope, and provided resource expropriation continued in Zaire, there was no core US interest in the continent.[4] Kissinger dreamed sometimes of a Pretoria, Nairobi and Cairo alliance. Lagos was included on occasions. However, this was Kissinger in his 'poles of power' musings, hangovers from his Harvard days when he conceived the world in terms of power and the logistical anchors that power required.[5] By and large, Kissinger

3. Henry Kissinger, *The White House Years*, London: Weidenfeld & Nicolson, 1979.
4. On the importance of the shipping route, see Larry Bowman, 'The Strategic Importance of South Africa to the United States: An Appraisal and Policy Analysis', *African Affairs*, vol. 81, no. 323, 1982.
5. Henry Kissinger, *A World Restored: Europe after Napoleon: The Politics of*

was happy if the Chinese wanted to play in Africa, and, in so far as the Chinese made Soviet interests in Africa problematic, welcomed it. The Chinese in Africa were not seen as a threat to Western interests just three decades ago.

So, some years after the end of the Cold War, with the West slow to recover from its triumphalism at having 'won' that war, the sudden perception of the Chinese posture in Africa was a shock. The sense of shock has coloured analyses ever since, so that much that has been written over the last ten years is alarmist. Not much of it is aware of the Cold War period of the Chinese African adventure. When it seeks to become aware, analysis is in terms of the Western political concerns of those days, just as it is in terms of Western economic concerns today. The Chinese are not accorded philosophical reasons for wanting to be in Africa and, above all, the Africans are accorded no agency of their own. Africa is depicted as an undifferentiated continent that can do nothing but await courtship and penetration by others. This essay is couched, therefore, as a personal journey, but is also concerned with philosophy and agency. These do not remove political and economic considerations but add to them. They make the relationship between China and Africa properly complex.

A global outlook from withdrawn enclaves

Four initial points need to be made. First, emphasis on China in Africa is often at the expense of a view of China in the world. China is rising as a global player. On visits to Beijing it is impossible to avoid a 'now it's our turn' self-assurance. The instant the view is widened, Africa becomes only one part of a complex Chinese global strategy – a valuable but not necessarily

---

Conservatism in a Revolutionary Age, New York: Grosset & Dunlap, 1964.

overwhelming part.[6] Second, Western views of China in Africa are often constructed by Sinologists who are not Africanists, or Africanists who are not Sinologists, or by Africanists and Sinologists who are not expert in international relations or international political economy, or international relations scholars who know nothing about either China or Africa. Blind or partially sighted people are describing the parts of the elephant they can feel. Third, such Chinese scholarly commentary that exists on Africa tends to observe Party lines closely. That is a necessity for career advancement, even career security, and to obtain funding for research in Africa. However, Chinese academic research in Africa can be extremely superficial and parochial. It tends to seek answers from officials of the African governments of the day. There is no wider political ethnography.[7] In so far as academic research makes any contribution to Chinese policy towards Africa (and it is only a third stream input), it suggests Chinese policy that doesn't always know what it is doing. Western observers who seek to comprehend Chinese African policy by studying the work of Chinese academics (and there are very few such Western observers) can reveal nothing of substance. Fourth, if there is a key objective in Chinese global economic policy it is to secure indisputable inroads into the European and US economies. The readiness, if not enthusiasm, to purchase American toxic debt in the economic meltdown of 2008-09 is an indication of the Chinese wish to own not only African resources, but key Western fiscal levers.[8] Economic leverage over the USA is more important than access to oil in

6. William Wallis, 'Drawing Contours of a New World Order', *Financial Times*, 24 January 2008.

7. See, as representative, *The Symposium of China–Africa Shared Development*, Beijing: Bureau of International Cooperation, 2006.

8. Jamil Anderlini and Henry Sender, 'An Embarrassment of Riches, albeit "Unreal"', *Financial Times*, 18 January 2011.

Africa. With leverage, everything else becomes possible anyway. In many ways, the Chinese should be exceptionally happy at all the emphasis on their profile in Africa - perfect camouflage.

As it is, figures relating to trade patterns reveal just how much emphasis on Africa skews the overall Chinese global profile. Over an eighteen-year period, 1992–2010, South African trade with China (all imports and exports) rose from 1.8 per cent of the South African total to 13.1 per cent. Nigerian trade with China rose from 0.5 per cent to 6.9 per cent. Egyptian trade rose from 1.6 per cent to 9.0 per cent. The key in these three African cases is that in none does trade with China represent anything close to a majority portion, or even approach a quarter of total trade volume. However, the percentages increase when looking elsewhere. US trade with China increased from 3.5 per cent to 14.3 per cent. Brazil's trade increased from 0.9 per cent to 14 per cent. The pattern throughout the most powerful trading nations of South Asia and Southeast Asia indicate 2010 volumes of 10.5 per cent (India) to 16.3 per cent (Malaysia) trade with China. However, it is the East Asia/Pacific basin that reveals the greatest percentage volumes of trade in 2010 with China. Here they do begin to approach the quarter mark: Japan 20.4 per cent, Taiwan 22.1 per cent, South Korea 22.8 per cent and Australia 20.6 per cent. The trading volume of an economically advantaged country like South Africa is analogous to that of Saudi Arabia (12.8 per cent), and Nigeria's is smaller than that of Russia (8.9 per cent).[9]

Of course, trade figures tell only part of the story. Overall Chinese foreign direct investment in Africa is growing at an increasing rate. But the original ambitions of the Chinese

---

9. Geoff Dyer, David Pilling and Henry Sender, 'A Strategy to Straddle the Planet', *Financial Times*, 18 January 2011; see also the chart in *African Business*, March 2008, p. 24.

leadership, as outlined below, were to gain the wherewithal to trade globally and successfully. FDI to secure expropriation rights is to ensure materials and inputs for the Chinese manufacturing sector, and it is income and profits from trade in manufactures that underpin the Chinese outlook for the future – no matter how much of an effort is made to diversify the market by greater internal consumption.

But external trading and FDI relationships need to be crafted on a carefully researched basis. A note on my third point, above, to do with academic work on Africa: this work, such as it is, takes its place alongside political reportage from Chinese embassies. The Chinese embassy model, however, is of fortress diplomatic enclosures. Staff live and work on site. The junior officials might as well be prisoners. Even senior diplomats confine themselves to government contacts. The embassy in Harare had nothing original to say to Beijing about Morgan Tsvangirai when he morphed from defeated opposition leader to prime minister. The Chinese had never talked to Tsvangirai. If Thabo Mbeki's vexed mediation did nothing else, it should have taught the Chinese a lesson in broadening political contact and reportage. However, even embassy reportage is subordinated to Party deliberations. The foreign affairs committees and organs of the Party, with their own research and deliberative apparatus, determine policy. The PLA (People's Liberation Army) has a powerful input on African issues, especially now that the Chinese have committed themselves to peacekeeping in arenas like Sudan, but it is an input to the Party. Chinese policy on Africa comes, essentially, from the Party.[10] No one outside really knows how the Party works. Watching the Chinese Communist Party requires skills that make Cold War Kremlinologists seem infantile. These

---

10. This is from early times: Gerald Segal, 'The PLA and Chinese Foreign Policy Making', *International Affairs*, vol. 57, no. 3, 1981.

points are all by way of context and caveat. This essay seeks to be bold, but it is hard to be unconditionally bold about anything Chinese these days.

Today's Chinese global outlook originates from Deng Xiaoping's four great economic modernizations of 1978 – although these were based on work initiated by Zhou Enlai as early as 1963. These were not simply to render a transition, within China, to a freer market economy, but to render China a participant in the economies of the wider world. The emphasis was largely internal in the first instance as, in the 1970s, there was no Chinese capacity to compete with the West. The idea was to build a base. From that base there would be expansion. Deng's idea was to purchase foreign industrial plant and machinery. The resulting products would form an export-led economic growth. In time, China would become one of the world's major trading powers. Until then, the Chinese were very much concerned to build bridges and forge alliances. This has been seen as political outreach but was as much an effort to form an international bloc of emerging economies which would become a strategic intersection between the West and the socialist economy of the Soviet Union. It was economic insurance, in case global trading power never came – or was successfully resisted – and it envisaged political leadership of a large part of the globe.

As with the four modernizations, the Chinese Three World Theory originated with Zhou Enlai – notably in his 1956 speech to the Bandung Afro-Asian summit – and this, in turn, was developed from Mao's 1946 interview with US journalist Anna Louise Strong. Mao told her that, between the two colossi of the United States and the Soviet Union, within the zone of imperial outreach by the USA and its resistance by the Soviet Union, was the rest of the world. The world was the target of struggle, its goal. By 1964, Mao had differentiated the zone in between as having two parts: developing nations, and what were basically the OECD nations outside the USA. It was Zhou's 1956 speech that suggested that not only was the world not bipolar, but that China would side with the middle zone, the world between, chiefly the Third World. By 1974, following China's disenchantment with the Soviet Union, the First World had become a conjoint imperial bloc encompassing both the USA and the USSR. The Second World comprised the developed nations outside the two great superpowers, and the Third World was developing. This was made official Party policy by Deng Xiaoping on 9 April 1974. Confucian protocol made it necessary to ascribe praise to Mao. Appropriately, in February 1974, when Zambia's President Kenneth Kaunda was visiting Beijing, Mao was said to have come up with the final formulation of the Three World Theory – inspired by the African leader.[11]

It was a neat trick, simultaneously Confucian (according Mao praise for the creation of the theory) and brotherly (even the theory's development owed to China's links with the developing world, in this case Kaunda). It also accorded respect to Africa since, at that time, Kaunda was regarded as a 'philosopher-king' figure. It was China saying to Africa that it did not believe the stereotype, created by Western colonialism, of the native without thought. The symbolism was carefully crafted for both internal and Third World consumption, and the Chinese got the symbolism right. The Three World Theory created space for the Chinese, and to this space it devoted money.

Well before 1974, however, as a result of Zhou's commitment at Bandung, Chinese largesse had begun to flow to Africa. In November 1956, only seven years after the Chinese Revolution, and after massive expenditure fighting in Korea, China made a

---

11. Herbert S. Yee, 'The Three World Theory and Post-Mao China's Global Strategy', *International Affairs*, vol. 59, no. 2, 1983.

US$4.7 million grant to Egypt. That was a huge amount for the 1950s. Even so, the Chinese were not always sure-footed. Zhou's 1965 tour of Africa was an unmitigated diplomatic disaster, in which the usually sure-footed Chinese premier succeeded only in putting his foot in his mouth. His people had certainly not helped him by failing to prepare the ground well, and that was a lesson it took the Chinese decades to learn – with academic research and embassy reportage even now, as noted above, failing to assist the Party leadership.

From 1970 to 1977, the Chinese spent some US$2 billion in Africa. This was half the Chinese aid budget. These were the years of the construction of the 550-mile Somalia border road; of the great Tazara Railway between Zambia and Tanzania, giving Zambia a transport route to the sea that was not at the mercy of the racist regimes in Rhodesia and South Africa. In some ways, it was the Tazara project that best epitomized the relationship China wanted with Africa. Workers from both continents laboured side by side. Zhou, calling for volunteers to go to Africa, warning that conditions were harsh and many would not return, had no difficulty with the numbers wanting to go. It was a romance in many ways – and that's the curious thing: despite all the self-interested calculation of Chinese benefit, there have been moments of pure idealism and romance. Africa, while well aware of Chinese interests, has never forgotten that idealism and romance.

It was precisely in the mid-1970s, however, that the contradictions in the Three World Theory became apparent. Siding with the Third World against the Soviet Union could not sit alongside fighting the Soviet Union's Third World allies. In the struggle for Angola that intensified with the precipitate departure of the Portuguese colonialists in 1975, China found itself on the side of the UNITA faction – along with the USA and South

Africa – while the Moscow-supported MPLA faction received the support of the Organisation of African Unity and, with decisive Cuban military intervention (financed by the Soviet Union), emerged victorious. It was also the decade where, alongside the more publicized Israeli assistance in the South African nuclear weapons programme, China covertly sold reactor-grade uranium to Pretoria.[12]

Descended from Confucius, powerless against the Soviets

The Three World Theory was a Chinese effort to gain leverage in world politics and, to a lesser extent, economics – and to give China leadership position among the developing countries. China wanted to become the acknowledged champion and *primus inter pares* of both the Non-Aligned Movement and the G77. It was to provide a platform from which China could forge alliances with the Second World of Europe and the non-American West. It was based in the hope that the First World, the imperial world of the two superpowers, would consume itself with its own rivalries, leaving China huge international freedoms. Not only did the First World not consume itself, the Chinese desire to lead the Third World relied upon no hostile Chinese action against those it 'led'. Angola and UNITA proved a difficult case. Even though the Chinese began withdrawing support from UNITA in 1976, with South Africa and the USA taking up the slack, its earlier assistance had helped make UNITA a fighting force that continued to destabilize Angola on a massive scale – right up to the battle of Cuito Cuanavale in 1984, which UNITA and the South Africans lost – and went on to remain a thorn in the

---

12. Stephen Chan, 'The Rise and Fall of the Chinese Three Worlds Theory – Chinese Foreign Policy and Africa', *The Round Table*, 296, 1985.

side of the Angolan Government until the death of the UNITA leader, Jonas Savimbi, in 2002.

Even though China extricated itself from supporting the wrong side in Angola, it found itself in an even worse position in 1979. When Vietnam, recently freed from American violence, began asserting its own regional interests in Cambodia, the Chinese became alarmed and invaded the country it had previously assisted. The Vietnamese dealt the Chinese a humiliating military blow – not a defeat as such, but the vaunted Red Army could not overcome opponents who had been hardened by years of fighting against 'superior' enemies. China withdrew, but had compromised its own Three World doctrine.

Far from being consumed in rivalry with the USA, the Soviet Union took the USA and the world by surprise with its 'out of a blue sky' unpredicted and full-strength invasion of Afghanistan in December 1979. The Chinese could not come to the aid of the Afghans, not even against a rival whom it had sought so assiduously to marginalize in the affections and interests of the Third World. It seemed that the Soviet Union could come and go exactly as it wished.[13]

Closer examination revealed other contradictions and flaws in the Three World Theory, and, although the theory was abandoned after the disasters of 1979, these flaws remain latent in all Chinese relationships with Africa. The key aspect is that, from the 1950s onwards, the Chinese felt they could and should be key in the struggles of the developing world. At the beginning of the 1950s they had come to the side of the North Koreans. By

---

13. On the Afghanistani and Soviet history, see Raja Anwar, *The Tragedy of Afghanistan: A First-hand Account*, London: Verso, 1988, with Fred Halliday's excellent Introduction; Stephen Chan and Dominic Powell, 'Reform, Insurgency and Counter-Insurgency in Afghanistan', in Paul B. Rich and Richard Stubbs, eds, *The Counter-Insurgent State: Guerrilla Warfare and State Building in the Twentieth Century*, Basingstoke: Macmillan, 1997.

Bandung in 1956, they had widened their remit to a global one. The Three World Theory of the 1970s simply tried to articulate 'philosophically' what the Chinese had been seeking to practise for twenty years. But there was a conceit in it. China was the key, China could be the leader, China had liberated itself first among the Afro-Asian nations. This begged questions about the position of Latin America, but, above all, it was assumed by the Chinese that they would be the international vanguard of liberation and emancipation. It was a curiously Leninist vision – except that China was hardly a small group of cadres leading the masses; China was huge. The contradiction was both in seeking to be the vanguard and being also the larger 'brother', the *older* brother, the brother who – in Confucian terms – had an unquestioned *responsibility* to lead the younger siblings; to be strong for them and, in return, receive their respect. What the Chinese gave and what they came to expect by way of receipts would prove problematic in Africa.

The idea that China was the older brother was an effort at a form of greater equality than the idea of China as a parent figure. But an older brother has certain leadership rights as well as responsibilities. It all works to a certain *politesse* descended from Confucius.

A short disquisition on vertical reciprocation[14]

Guanxi is best summarized as a Confucian doctrine of relationship and linkage. However, relationship is not static. There is a key dynamic quality embedded, and that is reciprocation. There must be two actors so that reciprocation can take place. Reciprocation becomes a relationship's mode of transaction.

14. For a slightly longer description of Chinese reciprocation, see Stephen Chan, 'A Chinese Political Sociology in Our Times', *International Political Sociology*, vol. 3, no. 3, 2009.

Four issues should be stressed at the outset. The first is that this renders the world of relationships a world of binaries. The second is that these binaries are not generally arranged in a horizontal relationship, but a vertical one. The third is that each vertically arranged binary is a metaphor of, and an expression derived from, a cosmic principle. Even the Chinese word for 'universe', *tien ha*, literally means 'heaven and earth', in which earth lies under heaven. Destiny and benefaction flow down; respect, worship and efforts to integrate with the flow of heaven make their way upwards. Fourth, reciprocation on earth is a tangible and physical act, or one with tangible and physical results.

Confucius proposed five sets of binaries and reciprocations within them: emperor and subject; husband and wife; father and son; older and younger siblings; and friend with friend. Only in the fifth was there a possibility of horizontal reciprocation. All reciprocations were, however, 'natural'. They have the same naturalness as Kant's moral universe, through *Recht*, establishing norms on earth among men. What made these teachings of Confucius revolutionary was that they provided for reciprocation that was natural, desirable and inescapable. It was a human responsibility to embrace them as one would embrace a natural state of affairs. It meant that the emperor himself had to reciprocate the allegiance of his subjects. He *had* to provide for them, look after them, fulfil their *right* to reciprocation. In this Confucian doctrine there was therefore no possibility of naked exploitation, and this becomes important in examining how the Chinese differentiate themselves from colonial and imperial powers in Africa. So that when Chinese officials begin their perorations on Africa with sermonesque reiterations of peace and friendship and assistance, they really mean it. The statements are not wool over eyes or naive self-deceptions. Expropriation may take place alongside or beneath the fine words, but expropriation is not exploitation. Expropriation demands a return – a reciprocation. It means, in practice, substantial front-loading of benefits to an African *partner* within a naturally vertical and naturally reciprocal relationship. The older sibling must provide. The younger sibling, by virtue of having been born afterwards, can only reciprocate after having first received a benefaction. Chinese behaviour can often be or seem outrageous in Africa – but very little of it escapes the Confucian *politesse* described here. This *politesse* would be inescapable even if the younger sibling had somehow been raised by barbarians and had developed barbaric attributes.

The outlands beyond the Central Kingdom

And Africa is indeed part of the traditionally 'barbarian' world – but so is the USA, Europe and everywhere else. As with all linguistic development, there is currently some revisionism in expressing the 'meaning' of various terms. They become 'modernized', sanitized and politically correct. So that traditionally pejorative Chinese terms describing foreigners – white ghosts and black devils for Europeans and Africans – are re-rendered as metaphors of other-worldliness, describing the alien world outside China, but not as insults. This is flimflam. They were condescending insults. In a way, they meant no more (or less) than, say, 'honkies' and 'niggers' – only no one says 'honkies' and 'niggers' anymore; however, popular speech in China still uses the old labels. The 'signified' may have outgrown the 'signifier', if the Chinese were to use the vocabulary of linguistic theory, but the signifier they use is still freighted with values and meaning that inflect perception.

The Chinese language cannot change easily. It has been the binding force of what is a hugely diverse nation for thousands of years. Even if spoken very differently in the far-flung parts of what is now China, the written language has remained a universal and unifying force. So that, even when spoken as different dialects, using different words, those words are both written in the same way and they *mean* the same thing. What is a tremendously unifying force is therefore also a tremendously conservative force. It cannot look forward to difference. It can only look backwards to speech and sign, to signifier, as it *was*. It looks backwards to an entire doctrinal and ideological foundation of centrality and unity. Beyond the circumference of the unified Middle Kingdom were only outlands.

The whole idea of the 'Middle Kingdom' was that it was the centre. 'Central Kingdom' might put it better; 'Core Kingdom' might put it best. Everything else rotated around it. In a sense, everything else was peripheral to it. Everything else could benefit from it, as both centre and periphery were described in terms not only of binaries, but of opposites. Civilized behaviour and virtuous ethics, balanced outlooks, the universe in harmony within Confucian values were contra-indicated by barbarian, illiterate, rebellious, disunited and unbalanced savageries. Highly developed culture, learning, technology and medicine were contra-indicated by things and people of nature – animalistic if not bestial, simple-minded, disease-ridden and capable only of subsistence technology. In this formulation, Africa becomes the world of nature and the good Confucian Chinese exercise virtue in seeking to 'balance' it with superior learning and technology.[15]

---

15. Qing Cao, 'Selling Culture: Ancient Chinese Conceptions of "the Other" in Legends', in Stephen Chan, Peter Mandaville and Roland Bleiker, eds, *The Zen of International Relations: IR Theory from East to West*, Basingstoke: Palgrave Macmillan, 2001.

But the outlands also evoke
high morality and romance

Having said that, the outlands are capable of recognizing the superior centre of the universe when they see it – even if it takes time. The Chinese ethos is not simply of condescension but of considerable romance in the way the worlds of culture and barbarity are balanced. I take great pleasure in the legend of Meng Huo, a Southern Chinese ruler – in the aeons gone by when Southern China was also regarded as a savage and barbarian place.

I remember that once, when I was working with an African delegation in Beijing, there was a daily historical epic on morning television. The delegation was sufficiently important for our accommodation to include waterproof plasma screens in the huge glass shower compartments. Being power-showered in the morning was for me, of Southern Chinese origin, a necessary mode of surviving the televised epic – in which the disciplined Chinese armies and heroes overcame Meng Huo's valiant but drunken rabble. The night before battle, all the northern soldiers are alert, ready, resting in a disciplined way for the morning showdown. Come the morning, they mount their horses in a thoroughly military fashion. Pan to the Southern encampment: Meng Huo is drinking much wine, mounting his concubine/s; and in the morning he almost mounts his horse backwards. He is at least portrayed as going down valiantly and repenting his sins before being magnanimously forgiven and incorporated into the great and growing China. Here is the story of Meng Huo. It is also a metaphor for Africa.

1. Meng Huo rebels against the rulers of the north, who already call their state the 'Middle Kingdom'. This shatters the region's balance of power.

2. Prime Minister Zhu is sent, with half a million soldiers, to crush Meng Huo.

3. Meng Huo is captured in the first great clash, but accuses the north of success by treachery. With great chivalry, Zhu sets Meng Huo free.

4. Zhu nevertheless sets about acquiring magical powers to neutralize the animalistic vigour of Meng Huo and his men.

5. Meng is captured a further five times, but each time pleads unfair capture and each time is released by the extremely virtuous Zhu.

6. On his seventh capture, Meng finally realizes he is being (consistently) defeated by someone who is not only superior militarily, but superior in virtue. When he realizes this, as in a sudden long-delayed revelation, he immediately capitulates.

7. His heart and mind won, Meng is allowed to remain as king of the south and becomes a steadfast ally and bearer of tribute to the Middle Kingdom. Equilibrium was thus restored by means of Zhu's virtue and patience.

What Zhu's equally patient soldiers would have made of this is unwritten. They were the ones laying down their lives, only to see their enemy released again and again. Virtue has its costs and its frustrations. It certainly costs great patience and persistence. China is prepared to work on Africa, despite any setbacks, for a very long time to come. This patience is reminiscent of Mao's favourite revolutionary ballet, *Taking Tiger Mountain by Strategy*. Sometimes frontal assault does not work. You can't just get it over and done with. Sometimes it's never quite done with. The televised epic I saw in Beijing never did have Meng Huo overcoming his taste in wine and concubines. Barbarians, even those adopted as younger brothers, never quite cease being barbarians.

Some outlands require not patience but pragmatism

The Three World Theory, as enunciated by Deng Xiaoping, was not reckless. Just as, in the early 1970s, Kissinger sought to detach China from residual solidarity with the international commitments of early Soviet ideology, so Zhou Enlai worked to ensure that China had a space for its own vision of commitments and rewards. Kissinger wanted a two-actor game – the USA and the Soviet Union – with China strong in itself but not a major actor in a global game of chess and balance of power. Zhou wanted a different two-actor game, with the USA and the Soviet Union united in their struggle against each other, and China free to sweep the rest of the world into its sense of strategic influence. For Africa and the developing countries, patience was required. Prime Minister Zhou was every bit as patient as Prime Minister Zhu. For the more developed, somewhat less barbaric Americans, Zhou needed great pragmatism and diplomacy. Kissinger was greatly impressed by Zhou, but he also knew that, beneath the diplomatic charm and worldliness, Zhou did not see him or his country as equals. In Kissinger's own words, Zhou possessed 'the sense of cultural superiority of an ancient civilization', and could skilfully soften 'the edges of ideological hostility by an insinuating ease of manner and a seemingly effortless skill to penetrate to the heart of the matter'. Kissinger also knew that, 'had China been stronger, it would not have pursued the improvement of relations with us with the same single-mindedness.'[16] The space that China sought, in order precisely to grow stronger, was in the Third World. Kissinger and Zhou established the Sino–US

---

16. There are now late musings by Kissinger on his and the US relationship with China; but for a Chinese account of the meeting between him and Zhou, see Kuo-kang Shao, *Zhou Enlai and the Foundations of Chinese Foreign Policy*, Basingstoke: Macmillan, 1996, pp. 202-3.

rapprochement in 1972–73. Deng Xiaoping announced the Three World Theory in 1974.

Rapprochement with the USA was a form of insurance against the Soviet Union, and allowed China some sense of security when it sought to bypass the Soviets in international relations. In so far as these relations concerned the Third World, the strategy was clear. In so far as they concerned the Second World, it was unclear. The Sino–US rapprochement allowed China space in East Asia. This was taken to mean Vietnam, Cambodia and Laos. It did not mean Japan, and it did not mean forcible intervention in Taiwan. But Japan was part of the Second World that China was supposed to win over – alongside Europe and Oceania. Again, there was no real mention of Latin America, and not much on Canada. The Chinese 'Worlds' were curiously incomplete. But, even within the Second World, influence and leadership could be impossible. China's long-standing grudge against Japan, greatly amplified by the events of the twentieth century and above all in World War II, meant Japan was both an economic rival and an impossible political partner. A Sino–Japanese economic pact would sweep the world. The foundations for that should have been laid in the 1970s, and were not. There was a limit to pragmatism. In a very real sense, Africa was the easy touch.

After the demise of the Three World Theory its conceits were still apparent: the sense of Chinese centrality and, increasingly as its economy grew, of destiny; the sense of Africa needing assistance but, now, with Chinese industrial growth having its own burgeoning needs, also the planned project of securing materials from Africa; the sense of providing assistance like an older brother in return for materials; but a curious sense, especially evident in the private Chinese entrepreneurs who saw Africa as a place in which they could make their fortunes, of condescension and racism.

This was all genuinely mixed with romance and also loyalty. In the days when China was a pariah, Sudan was the fourth African country to grant it diplomatic recognition. When al-Bashir's Sudan became a pariah, China repaid the debt of loyalty. This is a trait that exists in China's non-African relations. Its steadfast reluctance to condemn North Korea, while frequently vexed and deeply concerned about its behaviour – especially with regard to the nuclear programme and attitudes towards the South – is very much descended from the shared blood that flowed in the 1950s' Korean War against the USA. Beijing professor Zhu Feng has said that 'most Chinese have been immersed in an almost morbidly sentimental connection with the North', and there is still a powerful voice from the Chinese veterans of the Korean war. Tens of thousands of Chinese soldiers threw themselves into this war, and died. Legends have been made of their courage.[17] But perhaps Zhu Feng has chosen the right word: that combination of romance and loyalty is sentimental. It is powerfully sentimental. It should not be forgotten that, the atrocities of the Japanese against the Chinese people aside, the West also humiliated China in the Opium Wars, in the successful acquisition of 'free' port cities where the Chinese remit no longer ran, in the crushing of the so-called Boxer Rebellion, and in the militarized guarantee given to Taiwan. There is a point to prove against the West, but in the meantime Chinese sentimentality enables an identification with African struggles against colonialism and white minority rule.

Simultaneously, this is counterpointed with a different sentimentality – of China identifying with China. The great *gum san* of the early twentieth century, what the West calls the Gold Rush and the Chinese call the Gold Mountain, when people went to wild lands to look for their fortunes, helped build China. In my paternal grandfather's brigand-torn village, four watchtowers equipped with Browning machine guns were built on the remittances sent home from the gold miners. My maternal grandfather 'struck it rich' and built in his village a home which had an elevator. This was all lost with the Japanese invasion at the beginning of World War II, but the tales of the outside world, of the *mei guo*, the Beautiful Kingdom (the USA) and other strange lands, finally brought some exotica into the self-conceited Chinese imagination. China became a far-flung diaspora as well as the centre of gravity. In some respects, and notwithstanding the condescension, starting with Zhou Enlai's call for volunteers to help Africa with the Tazara Railway, Africa is a new exotica, in some ways also a new *gum san*.

The conditional future

The future is conditional because, as noted above, it is articulated in terms of a language constructed in the past and intended for past meanings of unity. The great Sinologist Jenner calls this 'the tyranny of history'.[17] That means a conservatism that is highly suspicious of dissent. This means that the language of dissent is a curious thing: it either partakes of the language of rule, of order, the 'natural' state of things in a unified structure; or it wishes either to rip that language apart, or substitute a new language for it, or bypass the order which the language typifies. It is almost impossible to explain this to people without some knowledge of the Chinese language. In terms of examples, however, the 1989 confrontation between students and authorities at Tienanmen Square was regarded as a tragedy – not only because the peaceful student protest was prematurely and unnecessarily crushed, but because no negotiation had been possible. The

17. W.J.F. Jenner, *The Tyranny of History: The Roots of China's Crisis*, London: Allen Lane, 1992.

students and authorities had been talking *past* each other, but using the *same* sort of language. Both claimed a Chinese form of 'categorical imperative', mandate of Heaven, righteousness in terms of tradition. It was a 'debate' over who owned what in the order of things and, particularly, the hierarchy of things.[18] When it was clear the students were claiming that they no longer felt constrained by the Confucian sense of deference to higher authority, but were deferring to even higher authority – the values of Heaven – the Party felt it no longer had to be constrained by obligation to 'younger brothers and sisters' – and killed them.

By contrast, a group like the Falun Gong disowned everything the Party and state represented. It didn't oppose them. They simply became unimportant in terms of what the sect called *fa* or Buddhist law. There is absolutely nothing original about the teachings: a typically eclectic Chinese confabulation of religious, meditational and physical stylistics.[19] In that sense, they should represent no danger. No sedition is preached. If it were a style of religion practised by small mountain communities nothing would have been done about it. Because its message became popular in the cities, and was perceived not as a challenge to the Party, but an even more radical non-recognition of the importance of the Party, dialogue became impossible. Western commentators often miss the point.[20] It is not that the Party set out to crush the Falun Gong. It does now, and often with great

---

18. Rudolf Wagner, 'Political Institutions, Discourse and Imagination in China at Tiananmen', in James Manor, ed., *Rethinking Third World Politics*, London: Longman, 1991.

19. See the writings of the sect's founder: Li Hongzhi, *China Falun Gong*, Hong Kong: Falun Fo Fa, 1998; Li Hongzhi, *Zhuan Falun*, Hong Kong: Falun Fo Fa, 1998.

20. Although they are perfectly correct about the brutality of suppression: Danny Schechter, *Falun Gong's Challenge to China: Spiritual Practice or 'Evil Cult'*, New York: Akashic, 2000; David A. Palmer, *Qigong Fever: Body, Science and Utopia in China*, London: Hurst, 2007; and, for a personal account of persecution, Gao Zhisheng, *A China More Just: My Fight as a Rights Lawyer in the World's Largest Communist State*, San Diego: Broad, 2007.

brutality. It is that the Party wanted to be existent and sentient and meaningful in the social recognitions of the sect. It wanted the sect to declare a place in a Confucian hierarchy, atop which the Party sat.

The Party also did not want the possibility of future challenge from the Falun Gong, along the lines of the Dalai Lama's challenge in Tibet, or, more to the point of historical precedence, the uprising of the Taiping in the nineteenth century – admired by Mao as a precursor to the Communist uprising a century later[21] – but this was a nationwide uprising based on a religious eclecticism that took the country by storm. Thinking back ensured there could be no alternative thinking forward.

The world outside China is also seen in terms of the needs, interests and history of China. In a modernized, technologized way, the Middle Kingdom still exists – and is concerned about the control of encroaching technology, its battles with Google being a case in point. The electronic artefacts of the outside world, barbarian and diasporic, can now come *in*. They at least make the Tienanmen slaughter impossible to repeat. In 1989, escaping protesters sent out grainy and unclear photographs on fax machines. One fax reached one number. The faxed images became less and less clear as the recipient sent it on – to one other number at a time. These days, instantaneous 'citizen broadcasting', websites, blogs, Twitter reach millions at a keystroke – with crystal clear images accompanied by sound and 'real time' immediacy. As in Tehran, the despatch of ringleaders will have to be done by executions far from cameras. But, if the possible mass of future protesters is 'safe', what language will it speak to power? Maybe net language, text and Twitter abbreviations will erode the backwards power of the Chinese language. But at what

21. For pointers on the Taiping's place in a radical genealogy, see Jonathan D. Spence, *The Chan's Great Continent: China in Western Minds*, New York, Norton, 1998.

point in the spectrum of past referents and future hopes will there be a conjuncture for negotiation? At some stage, the Middle Kingdom may well find itself infused with fissure lines.

To a large extent, the future of China–Africa relations will change when African websites and Africa-originated communications start penetrating Chinese interest. At least private entrepreneurs will no longer go out to Africa with the appalling mix of naivety, ignorance and assumed superiority they so often take with them now. Africa will be less predated upon when it speaks, itself, in modern global terms and via global means. Not only the Chinese will receive this new speech. It will enter the world at large and even China will have to partake of a new global recognition and discourse of a changing Africa. Until then, the recent history of China and Africa has had its fair share of brazen stupidities, cupidities and deliberate blindness.

Zambia and the copper mountain

Not a *gum san*, or gold mountain, but a copper one, Zambia has attracted much international penetration, investment and acquisition. Before Chinese private entrepreneurs began buying copper mines in Zambia, foreigners of many nationalities did so – the Indians being the generation just before the Chinese. However, whereas the Indians and others tended to asset-strip, whatever the faults of Chinese management, Chinese ownership sought to revive the productivity of the mines and to take advantage of a rising spike in world prices for the mineral.

The new generation of mine managers was very much a third-generation diaspora. A small group of workers on the Tazara project had settled in Zambia, and there was some subsequent modest migration of Chinese personnel from other parts of the region – for example, Angola – as the Chinese role there wound

down, and some residue from Chinese aid projects. The generation of the 2000s was the first fully entrepreneurial, as opposed
to idealistic, influx of Chinese. They didn't have a clue. The tiny
diasporic community that was already in place, although tending
to live within its own enclaves, was horrified.

The Chinese residents were themselves mindful of the considerable goodwill left by the Tazara project. Declared uneconomic
and logistically too difficult by Western interests, the 1,158-mile
railway between Zambia and Tanzania, designed to give Zambia
a relief-line to the sea – to reduce dependence on lines that ran
south through apartheid territory – was a major engineering feat.
It never worked well. However, the sheer scale of the effort and,
above all, the *willingness* to attempt it, and to sacrifice for it,
made a huge impact on the beleaguered Zambians – who were
incurring great losses to support liberation movements in Rhodesia and South Africa, and whose export routes through exactly
these countries could be strangled at a moment's notice. In 1970,
China pledged an interest-free $406 million loan for the railway
and, with both Chinese and African labour, it was completed
in 1976. The propaganda films from this period, despite their
propagandistic intent and techniques, are still moving. It *was*
moving. Anyone who was actually involved would say so.

In the years afterwards, China embarked on its internal
modernization project and moved to develop its capitalist
model. When, in the 1990s and 2000s, Zambia also liberal-
ized its economy, this conjunction permitted a new form of
Chinese interest and investment.[22] It was an interest alongside
those of others. Legions came to exploit what Zambia offered,
but the Chinese effort was sometimes under-researched and

---

22. Muna Ndulo, 'Chinese Investments in Africa: A Case Study of Zambia', in Kweku
Ampiah and Sanushu Naidu, eds, *Crouching Tiger, Hidden Dragon: Africa and China*,
Durban: University of KwaZulu Natal Press, 2008.

sometimes thoughtlessly crude. Not always: the revitalization in the 2000s of infrastructure such as the hydroelectric plant at Kafue Gorge, and the establishment of the Solwezi-based Lumwana Power Project, have considerably boosted Zambian energy supply and reliability. Moreover, Chinese state-owned enterprises have usually gone about their investment within joint ventures, albeit as majority shareholders: Qingdao Textiles formed Zambia-China Mulungushi Textiles Joint Venture Ltd, on a 66 to 34 per cent ownership basis, with the Zambian Ministry of Defence. China Nonferrous Metal Industries, through its Non Ferrous Company-Africa subsidiary, bought 85 per cent of the almost defunct Chambishi copper mine. These initiatives turned what many regarded as basket cases into productive concerns. China is now the third largest provider of FDI in Zambia, after South Africa and the UK.[23]

The *operational* aspects of Chinese majority ownership, however, have continued to be a disaster. At Chambishi mine in 2005, forty-nine miners were killed in an explosion. The safety procedures under Chinese management immediately came under question, and the matter became a major issue in the Zambian elections of 2006, when the leading opposition candidate Michael Sata threatened to repudiate ties with China and open them with Taiwan.[24] Notwithstanding the politicization of the mining question, in 2007 Chinese guns were turned upon protesting workers at the same mine. In 2008, a Chinese manager of a copper smelter was beaten up by Zambian workers seeking better conditions. In 2009, the Zambian government introduced legislation that purportedly forced Chinese mine owners to observe minimum safety and

23. For an excellent compilation of cases and data, see Lucia Ribacchi, *Chinese in Africa: Investors or 'Infestors'? Evidence from the Case Study of Chinese Investments in Zambia*, M.Sc. dissertation, School of Oriental and African Studies, London, 2010.

24. I was in Zambia at the time, covering the election.

environmental standards. However, in October 2010, Chinese supervisors shot thirteen protesting miners at the Collum coal mine. Immediately, both the Zambian government and the Chinese embassy ordered settlement of the dispute in favour of the miners, and the supervisors were arrested. The Collum mine was owned by private Chinese entrepreneurs, but they had not learned the harsh lessons that the Chinese state-owned Nonferrous group had been taught at Chambishi. Put in a nutshell, the Chinese managers imagined that pirate operating procedures, drawn from practice in China itself, would suffice in a barbaric African country. Even more to the point, a huge number of Chinese managers have refused to integrate with their workers and have resorted to bullying and guns out of unmitigated racism. This became an election issue in 2011. The opposition leader, Michael Sata, observed at the time of Collum: 'I can't see any investor in the People's Republic of China shooting any Chinese and getting away with it.' Here, he was not only referring to racist mismanagement, but also making a critique of how official relationships between China and Zambia militate against ensuring that private companies abide by legal standards. Part of the complaint in many countries is how Chinese entrepreneurs behave as if outside the law.

Notwithstanding the appalling nature of such racist management, there is a key distinction to be made. The macro-*intent* of Chinese FDI, and as intended also by its state-owned enterprises, has certainly been to maximize production and returns, but *also* to accomplish some infrastructural and productive good in Zambia. Poorly trained, poorly briefed and determinedly un-acculturated managers – working all the same to merciless targets – have meant gross operational shortcuts and neglect of health and safety requirements that were on the books well before the 2009 additional legislation in Zambia. In many ways, Zambia is the most labour-legislated country in Africa. Its record of signing up to ILO conventions is remarkable. Observation has often, however, been patchy and the Chinese have sought to participate in the glossing over of standards. When, however, cheating is accompanied by late payment of salaries, unreasonable working practices and racism, the Chinese have only themselves to blame for devising a noxious and toxic cocktail. Nevertheless, operational mismanagement has been used as a hatchet to attack China's overall strategic intent towards providing local as well as Chinese benefits. Some of that intended local benefit was writ large in an audacious proposition, resisted strenuously by the West, in the Democratic Republic of the Congo.

The copper mountain and universities

The *da xue* (Mandarin: the big study, or the big reading) or *dai ho(k)* (Cantonese: the big learning) are Chinese terms for a university. *Da* or *dai* is a very generic term. Although usually translated as 'big', it can also mean 'great'. In this case, I prefer the translation 'grand'. Thus: the grand learning. In the romance of the 'old days', learning was the only way to bypass the class system. The annual imperial exams allowed even the poorest subject to step outside his poverty and feudal status to become an official. The successful candidates would be given a red robe of rank, a mortar board with tassels not unlike the later Western version, and be paraded in his home town on a white horse. He was of course also given a government job, but all these advantages had been gained deservedly because of grand learning. When, later, learning became concentrated in universities, the institutions became prestigious and symbolic. They were the portals of escape.

With this in mind, it is amazing that Chinese aid to Africa has not earlier seized upon the building of universities. The addition of universities was what was unremarked about the original Chinese proposal for the Democratic Republic of the Congo (DRC) in 2008. China pledged a $9 billion loan, $3 billion of which was to develop mines, over which China entered a 68 to 32 per cent joint venture involving Sinohydro Corporation and DRC's previously almost defunct Gecamines; and $6 billion was for infrastructure, with China Railway Engineering Corporation playing a major role. The Chinese expected to gain 6.8 million tons of copper and 620,000 tons of cobalt over a twenty-five-year period. However, China would also build huge expanses of road and railway and, along those transport routes, a large number of clinics, schools and universities.[25] It was an unheard-of proposal; it would have transformed development in the south of DRC, with provision for a huge increase in the national pool of trained personnel; and it thoroughly alarmed the West, which saw an exponential increase of Chinese influence in Central Africa.

Using the IMF as a battering ram, and insisting upon the priority of its own development assistance programme, the West succeeded in reducing the Chinese package to $6 billion.[26] At the time of writing, it is unclear how many elements of infrastructure have been sacrificed in this reduction. But what it still means is 2,400 miles of road, 2,000 miles of railway, 32 hospitals, 145 health centres and two universities. I use this provision to make the obvious point that on this occasion there was a keen symmetry between Chinese and African aspiration – and this included both the benefits and the prestige of higher education. Western assistance has always prioritized primary

25. Tim Whewell, 'China to Seal $9 bn DR Congo Deal', *BBC News*, http://news.bbc.co.uk/go/pr/fr/-/1/hi/programmes/newsnight/7343060.stm, 14 April 2008.

26. Antonaeta Becker, 'DRC Forced to Downsize Deal', *News Africa*, vol. 1, no. 97, 30 June 2010.

schooling, but the Chinese approach in this instance recognized something beyond foundational competencies. It recognized the need for educational foundations for international competitiveness – albeit in a distant future. In the meantime, it recognized the psychological foundation a university degree confers in situations of underdevelopment. The graduate is credentialized as having escaped the structural constraints of poverty upon his or her capacity to understand and interrogate the world. In the backwaters of southern Democratic Republic of Congo, this has the psychological impact of a huge achievement.

What is this distant future?

There is a key asymmetry in the negotiating capacities of African and Chinese governments. This resides in the fact that few African officials speak Chinese. African governmental penetration of Chinese thought and preparation, of such research as is available to the Chinese public, and the capacity to understand preparatory and tactical chatter within Chinese delegations, is weak. The Chinese themselves have funded Confucius Institutes in a small but growing number of locations, but their language teaching is not widely subscribed. There is no push to learn Chinese in Africa, and in any case normal Chinese pedagogies in language teaching are appallingly out of step with modern approaches and technologies. You won't get interactive computer programmes that teach young people, for instance, how to flirt in Chinese. Besides, Heaven forbid that African youths should flirt with Chinese girls! There is still a combined residual racism and puritanism there. And the insistence that language must be taught in its spoken and written forms simultaneously is not helpful. It brings together two ridiculous difficulties: the first is mastery of the pronunciation cadences; and the second is that, even with modern simplified script, rote learning is required for hundreds of basic characters and thousands of others with more sophisticated meanings or possibilities. There is an additional, third difficulty. Chinese is not as precise and rational a language as English and French; and its analogical characteristics differ from those of many African languages that are, often, also grammatically more complex than Chinese. But, although there are real reasons why learning Chinese is unattractive, in addition to the fact that its learning is not particularly incentivized for individual students, all this does mean yet another generation of African negotiators at disadvantage.

Where there is symmetry is recognition of what artefacts the future should hold for Africa. In the 1980s there was a brief fascination in many African policy circles with the experiment in North Korea. This was partly because of the impressive propaganda tours offered by the North Korean government at that time, together with the paraphernalia of honours and medals bestowed upon the official visitors. But what seemed genuinely impressive was the cradle-to-grave welfare system, state-originated and managed, not requiring any development of civil society and other intermediaries between state and citizen, and all couched – in those pre-electronic-revolution days – in the latest that mechanical and civil engineering technology could offer. The two aspects that attracted attention were very much the obviation of the need for an intermediate zone of organization between state and citizen, and the sense of industrialized modernity. This was at the time that the West was talking about 'basic needs' as the developmental path forwards for Africa.

To an extent, the West has returned to the 'basic needs' template – that the emphasis should be on clean water, housing and the like. 'Assured subsistence' might be another coinage. The current emphasis on Millennium Development Goals is a sophisticated development of this template, and gender equality is really the only key addition and difference. The goals are not only a set of targets; they constitute a ceiling. The aim is very much to ensure a level of development that prevents slippage into underdevelopment; it is not to take any part of Africa into a millennium in which, like China, it challenges the West. The West is not providing aid to develop a competitor. Nor are the Chinese. But the image of China, precisely as a competitor to the West, is a deeply attractive one. So China as a developed economic and technological power is an aspirational model. What this aspiration envisages in Africa is the right to manufacture, to the industrialization of products, to beneficiation. By and large, the Chinese are not providing this, just as the West did not. However, in so far as joint ventures might be possible between such African industrial concerns that exist and Chinese ones, the outlook for cooperation in automotive manufacture in South Africa is, while hardly consolidated, a prospective one. So that when the West looks upon current Sino-African relations with alarm, it should be mindful that, perhaps, it is alarmed by a stage one, and might be even more alarmed by the possibility of a stage two. This stage could not, as noted, provide competition with China, but it could in certain sectors provide competition with the West. The processing of coffee and cocoa, for instance, would not compete with Chinese concerns but would destabilize processing plants in Europe.

The upward spiral of this moves on to petroleum refineries across all African oil producers, but also local build of pipes for pipelines.[27] Chinese assistance with steel plants is a key outlook for the future. But these would be best suited to joint ventures, and this would require the upgrade of local capacities as well as

---

27. All a part of a global competition: Dino Mahtani, 'The New Scramble for Africa's Resources', *Financial Times*, 28 January 2008.

local investment. It would also require, as cooperation became more sophisticated, shared senior management. A working joint Sino-African company board of a major enterprise would have to become more than a rare event.

Chinese weaknesses and vulnerabilities[28]

There are two common assumptions in extant literature on China and Africa. The first is that Africa is of critical and primary importance to China and its drive to grow and industrialize. The second is that China is unrestrained in its largesse to Africa, is at ease with this largesse, and sees no risks in it. Both assumptions are false. Here, I wish to outline a key number of fault lines and risks in the Chinese approach to Africa, and misconceptions about the Chinese approach.

First, there is a misconception that Africa is China's most important area in its global outreach. As I have said, this is not true. Although all parts of Beijing's outreach can be seen as interrelated and interdependent, those that are priorities at this time are better trade relations, especially trade entry, with Europe; and increasing economic leverage with the United States. Leverage through buying toxic debt, in making investments across a range of enterprises and properties, and in maintaining exchange rates that are favourable to China are what China finds important. In a sense, the misconception of Africa's prime importance to China is a Western construction. The major preoccupation of the West in this regard is to do with Chinese access to oil - particularly to energy sources in a future when Middle Eastern supply will no longer be enough for the West.

28. This section is a refinement and elaboration of points I make in Stephen Chan, 'Ten Caveats and One Sunrise in Our Contemplation of China and Africa', in Alden, Large and Soares De Oliveira, eds, *China Returns to Africa*.

If oil was not in the picture, the West would not have expressed such concerns over China in Africa. It has nothing to do with Africa. It has everything to do with two giants needing access to sources of energy.

Second, there is no single Chinese profile in Africa. Although there is a basket of major countries in which there is Chinese interest and commitment – Angola and Sudan (North and South) would be in this basket – there is a felt need to build links in particular with South Africa and, to a lesser extent, but still a greater extent than with other countries, Nigeria. These two have the largest GDPs and, especially in the case of South Africa, the most variegated economic sectors. The more variegated the sector, the more avenues of cooperation there are. In other countries, the Chinese must first help build, if not build by themselves, entire areas of infrastructure and variegation. In all the African countries where it is present, the Chinese diaspora is varied and, in some countries, behaves more clumsily, if not despicably. Private Chinese citizens, seeking the *gum san* in Africa, can muddy the reception of even massive official Chinese assistance. The official Chinese still haven't developed a briefing and education programme for private migrants. This is very short-sighted. Finally, even when the chief concern is indeed to do with petroleum resources, there can be vast differences of approach. The Chinese are simply not as good at offshore drilling and technology as, for instance, the Europeans. In some areas, collaborative ventures will simply be more cost-beneficial and efficient. Different sorts of joint venture, both with local concerns and with other international actors, may well vary the African picture even more in the future.

Third, Chinese capacity in Africa is not manufactured out of nothing. The notion of an endless reservoir of Chinese resources is inaccurate. Investment in Africa, as with investment anywhere, is dependent on trade surpluses and earnings. It is dependent on exchange rates that favour China. It is in short dependent on the continuing Chinese capacity to dictate certain terms in its international economic dealings or, at least, to resist calls for amelioration of those terms. This is not to say that the Chinese are in anything but a strong position at the present time. China enjoys foreign exchange reserves of US$2,850 billion. It is the single largest foreign owner of US Treasury securities. However, having such reserves increases the pressure to invest. Liquidity cannot stay still and, in the dynamics of modern capitalism, the flow of capital is more important than its mere accumulation. But this means that investment has got to have 'secure' as well as 'risky' outlets. The USA is the significant 'secure' outlet in the Chinese portfolio. The US Treasury market is therefore a 'safe haven'. But this is a double-edged sword: it makes the USA dependent on Chinese liquidity, but it makes China vulnerable to US political pressures. It makes complex and varied the bilateral dynamics, and these dynamics will take much watching and attendance.

Fourth, the same applies to China's domestic economic base. Hitherto, the national savings base has been remarkable, and the state has access to this. However, as modern pressures continue to squeeze peasant productivity and savings potential, and as the stock market continues in its relatively under-regulated fashion – with both untoward swings in investment patterns and dangers of overheating – there can be no guarantee that the savings base will remain as stable as before. China has staved off the global recession by dramatic injections of finance into its domestic economy. It took a huge risk in doing so, but the very fact that it had to do so reveals that its economy is subject to both international pressures and national confidence.

It should also be said that there is significant Chinese public-sector debt. In addition, the workings of the internal Chinese capital market are not only given to dangers of overheating; they are a constant battleground between reformists and fiscal conservatives. Nothing about the Chinese economy is simple, and its absolute stability should not be taken for granted.

Fifth, Western concern over Chinese expansionism in Africa, in so far as it is centred on resource capture and particularly the capture of petroleum resources, is due to the West forseeing a future when Middle Eastern oil diminishes while the Western industrial machine continues to grow. African oil would be not a current but a future alternative. If that alternative has been pre-empted by the Chinese, then current balances in global economic power stand to be disrupted. But if African oil is the only viable future alternative for the West, then it is that also for the Chinese. To an extent, although very much future-based, the African seeds of Chinese success will also be its limitation. In short, outside Africa China has no analogous expansion programme. It has put its eggs in one, albeit large, basket.

Sixth, in concentrating on this basket the Chinese are taking incredible risks. It is as if there is often no, or very little, political risk analysis. The Democratic Republic of the Congo is simply not a stable country. Its recent volatility has been extreme. Its corruption is also extreme and its government has done little to facilitate genuine development. To an extent, especially in southern DRC, the Chinese will be doing this for the government. But this means close identification with the government and vulnerability to criticism if not attack by association. It may be that there is Chinese political risk analysis. It may be that it is predicated on a very long game with horizons that extend way beyond Western analysis. Western analysis dwells on entry conditionality, recouping of investment and start-up costs, recurrent budget profit margins in the short term and overall profits against investment in the long term. It would not be overgeneralizing to sketch a model of short- and long-term profits of ten years plus ten years – a two-decade scenario that is weighed against risk. The Chinese are likely to have a longer time frame, but then they are guessing the risk component. Certainly, their academic research inputs are incredibly limited and naive; the foreign ministry and its embassies are also operationally restricted – as noted earlier, embassies are walled enclaves and many operatives seldom leave the compound and very few interact with local people, except at the most senior levels. Final foreign-policy decisions are taken by Party committees. I have no idea of their information and analysis base (nor does anyone else) or how they configure risk. However, the entire Chinese expectation in Africa, repeated from country to country, is that either the governments with whom they deal will be sustained, or any successor government will sustain good relations with China. There seems to be no scenario plan that deals with being pre-emptorily asked to leave.

Seventh, either because of that lack of long-term surety, or in addition to it, the Chinese have thrown much political weight at the highest level into good relations with Africa. The Chinese president and prime minister are familiar visitors in many countries. Their presence is in contradistinction to the infrequent visits of senior Western leaders. They personify what they have put in place as a loosely labelled 'Shanghai' model, in contradistinction to a 'Washington' model, whereby Western-style conditionalities do not exist, and all assistance projects are front-loaded with visible benefits and conspicuous 'sweeteners'. The ability of Chinese corporations and the Chinese government to work intimately together means speed of operation and speed of agreement. It means huge reserves for investment and sweetener purposes. The Chinese model seems to combine political weight with economic largesse and to indicate constantly its difference from the clumsier, slower, less coordinated and conditionalized Western methodologies. But this commits the Chinese to this kind of high-profile and high-level and high-investment model come what may. Whatever the long-term benefits, it is a very expensive model.

And that leads lastly – and this is the eighth fault line – to a factor upon which few have remarked: that the 'Shanghai' model has two components that extend the horizon of risk to an extreme point. The first is the obvious fact that, in providing African countries with a new generation of loans, China takes a very much longer view of repayment time spans than the West did. But this also exposes the time frame to volatilities, defaults and repudiations. In any case, it means simply a very long time before repayment is complete. China therefore has 'exposure' in Africa. The second is the less obvious point that, in front-loading so many 'sweeteners' in any African country, China makes huge assumptions about that country's absorptive and operational capacities. Even if the Chinese do most of the initial implementation, building and finishing of facilities, what about maintenance, upgrade, coordination, criminal or rebel damage? And, where the Chinese do not do most of the initial implementation, what about the recipient country's capacity to do so? Will there be a key stage when the 'Shanghai' model appears to be throwing good money after bad? The methodology is often a gigantic leap of faith.

Slow but sure changes in the Chinese posture

Nothing stays the same. 'All that is certain is that there is tumult under Heaven.' This old saying was one of Mao's favourites and was also used by Deng Xiaoping. Even carefully devised and enunciated 'principles' can mutate. At the 1956 Bandung

Conference, Zhou Enlai announced the key principle of 'non-interference'. It has been a badge of Chinese relations with Africa, and dictator after dictator has been secure in the knowledge that the Chinese would not 'interfere' (in any public sense at least) with their political regime. It was a defence for continued Chinese cooperation with Sudan's al-Bashir at the height of the massacres in Darfur, west Sudan – and this was after the African Union had itself moved towards a principle of 'non-indifference' and was insistent upon a peacekeeping force being installed in Darfur.[29] However, behind the scenes, the Chinese had begun to negotiate and work with the government of South Sudan, until recently another antagonist of al-Bashir's regime in Khartoum. It was autonomous under the 2005 Comprehensive Peace Agreement that ended a civil war between North and South that had lasted a quarter of a century. These negotiations began years before the 2011 referendum that guaranteed independence for South Sudan, and were taking place even while President al-Bashir still had hopes of maintaining a union between North and South. The state-owned China National Petroleum Corporation (as a major partner in the Greater Nile Petroleum Operating Company consortium, which also includes Malaysia's Petronas Carigali Overseas, and India's ONGC Videsh) has a 40 per cent stake in the oil blocs that straddle the North/South border between the two Sudans. China saw the writing on the wall for the Sudanese union some time ago, and moved swiftly to establish its *bona fides* with the South.[30] Simultaneously, China's special envoy to Africa, also its special envoy to Darfur, Liu Guijin, was not only highly instrumental behind the scenes in

---

29. Although the Chinese did lighten considerably their stance over Darfur. This was characterized by several high-profile diplomatic visits at the highest level to Sudan. But there is a case to be made as well for some gentle and non-official diplomatic influence: Paul Moorcraft, *Inside the Danger Zones*, London: Biteback, 2010, pp. 396–8.

30. Geoff Dyer, 'Signals of a Shift', *Financial Times*, 21 January 2011.

persuading al-Bashir to allow the South to go; he should properly be credited with a key role in ensuring al-Bashir reduced the violence in Darfur. High-level visits to Sudan by Chinese leaders were only the public manifestation of work below the surface, and this work was conducted by Liu Guijin.[31] Liu is a diplomat of consummate skill and sophistication, so there are two things at work here: first, a very slow but apparent movement away from 'non-interference' as a cover-all principle or doctrine; and, second, the deployment for the first time of someone who knows what he is doing in Africa.

Greater pragmatism and more expertise? Time will tell. But, if there is, then will this make the West even more alarmed by China in Africa? The final word should be drawn again from Zhou Enlai's encounter with Henry Kissinger. Each man was greatly impressed by the other. Kissinger asked Zhou what he thought had resulted from the 1789 French Revolution. Zhou said that it was too soon to tell.

China, in its contemporary guise, has been working in, benefiting and expropriating from Africa since the 1950s, and certainly since shortly after the wave of sub-Saharan independences in the 1960s. Much of the current Western concern is not even a decade old. It has become a hurried, sometimes frenzied, speculative and somehow indecent addition to the scholarly 'industry' that now passes as scholarship itself. What I have tried to do, as a figure sometimes taken to personify a 'bridge' between Africa and China, is to inaugurate the sort of debate that scholars have not fully conducted, and to have as leading voices in that debate, beginning in the pages that follow, those interesting creatures that the Western debate has curiously and self-seekingly marginalized: the Chinese and Africans themselves.

---

31. The present author was able to discuss these matters privately with Liu Guijin in 2010.

PART II

Chinese responses

2

Sino-African cultural relations: soft power, cultural statecraft and international cultural governance

JERRY C.Y. LIU

Stephen Chan's wide-ranging essay on 'The Middle Kingdom and the Dark Continent: An Essay on China, Africa and Many Fault Lines' is characteristically authoritative and far-sighted. The argument is clear and accessible, the touch light. The case made, while carrying philosophical weight, has implications for the understanding of Sino–African relations that are pragmatic in nature. In order to explain Chinese political, economic and diplomatic behaviour in Africa, crucial questions are asked throughout the essay, engaging with the old and the new, the historical and the modern, the ideal and real. For me the key question is, can we speak of a Chinese mode of thinking informing its diplomatic relations, of a Chinese way of statecraft, in Africa? If so, how different is it from the European and US models in both philosophical and practical terms? Can we identify a consistent cultural or philosophical rationale behind the decision-making that shapes China's Africa strategy? Or, even if the rationale has not been thoroughly consistent, does it nevertheless reveal some discerning features of what Stephen Chan implies is the 'Chinese ethos' or Confucian way of statecraft, whose template differs philosophically and pragmatically from the realist approach of the West? Or are the Chinese in fact simply the same practical and interest-seeking creatures as Western envoys in Africa?

So, just how distinctive is Chineseness in its engagement with the African economy (from its expanding external trade relations, increasing foreign direct investment, interest-free loans, buying access to oil resources, long-term investment in infrastructure such as railroads, universities and hospitals, to its risk-taking entrepreneurship), and in its political leverage in the continent (i.e. from the Three Worlds Theory, the Non-Aligned Movement, the G77, non-interference policy, covert selling of reactor-grade uranium, to the installing of peacekeeping forces) as a whole? It is useful to return to the concept and practice of Chinese statecraft in history. First, in my view the phrase 'culturing Chinese statecraft' captures the Confucian way well. In the political sciences and real politics, culture is often taken as a marginal factor in explaining state behaviour. Cultural explanation is usually accorded less value than other forms. Yet, by referring to Chinese statecraft as 'culturing', we mean to establish the very clear influence of Confucian ethics and cultural values on the administration and management of traditional Chinese state bureaucracy, as well as its engagement in foreign affairs. Governments in China have historically manifested a peculiar degree of self-restraint (rarely emphasized in European records). It is fair to say that morality and virtue were closely associated with the legitimacy of state activities within and without China. Such self-restraint was reflected in Chinese states' idealistic principle of governing, which Confucius termed *weizheng yide*, 'to rule by virtue', or *renzhi*, the 'rule of benevolence'. By this Confucius meant that, instead of using political interest and criminal punishment as the standards of governance, rulers and politicians should 'guide people with virtue, and rule them with rites or courtesies'.

Through the Han to the Ming–Qing periods, this Confucian ethos was integrated tightly into Chinese intellectual traditions, the Confucian classics and the civil examination system. One need only read a few pages of Ming–Qing *jingshi* (lit. 'managing the world') literature to understand the powerful influence of culture on Chinese statecraft and foreign affairs. Understanding the concept of *jingshi* will help elucidate the context of Chinese official decision-making, for it differs in many ways from modern Western discourses of statecraft. First, the Chinese concept of statecraft includes not only foreign state policies and diplomacy, but also the rules and protocols informing the interior affairs of the state bureaucracy. For state politicians, foreign affairs are definitely a moral extension of domestic rule based on the principle of benevolence. Second, many scholars explain *jingshi* solely as the politics, administration and management of bureaucratic statecraft. Such interpretation indeed covers a very important aspect of the concept; however, Chinese statecraft involves more than that. It is an integral part of the Confucian value system, carrying within it the dual characteristics of classic learning: namely, the pragmatism and utilitarianism of 'practical statesmanship', on the one hand, and the pursuit of self-realization through absolute ethical ends that defines 'moral statesmanship', on the other.[1] During the late Ming and Qing periods, so-called '*jingshi* learning' included at once the study of classical moral philosophy and practical deeds, approaches to and sectors of rule (such as construction and transportation,

---

1. Hao Chang, 'On the Ching-shih Ideal in Neo-Confucianism', *Ch'ing-shih Wen-t'i*, vol. 3, no. 1 (1974); 丘為君, 張運宗, "戰後台灣學界對經世問題的探討與反省," 新史學, vol. 7, no. 2 (1996): 181–231, p. 195.

taxation, finance, personnel and security issues), and the administration of bureaucracy.

Before Prince Henry the Navigator of Portugal began in 1415 to carry out the plan so close to his heart, sending two or three ships every year to discover the African coast beyond Cape Nam,[2] the Chinese admiral Zheng He, commanding a fleet of 300 ships and over 20,000 men, had sailed across the Indian Ocean and the Arabian Sea and reached the eastern coast of Africa in 1405. Nonetheless, with a conquistador mentality the Portuguese took from Angola alone no fewer than 1,389,000 slaves between 1641 and 1486, an activity of which many occidental scholars approved. While the Portuguese east of Suez deemed themselves 'saviours of the pagans' and 'crusaders of Christ' who engaged in total war, the Chinese voyages were those of a well-disciplined navy paying friendly visits to foreign ports. In 1911 a stele commemorating one of the visits of the Ming navy under Zheng He was unearthed in the town of Galle. The inscription on the tablet provides a perfect illustration of the extension of the Chinese cultural ideal outside its territory:

> His Imperial Majesty, Emperor of the Great Ming, has dispatched the Grand Eunuch Zheng He ... to set forth his utterances before the [Lord] Buddha, the World-Honoured One, as herein follows... Of late we have dispatched missions to announce our Mandate to foreign nations, and during their journeys over the oceans they have been favoured with the blessing of Thy beneficent protection... Wherefore according to the Rites we bestow offerings in recompense, and do now reverently present before the [Lord] Buddha, the World-Honoured One, oblations of gold and silver, gold-embroidered jewelled banners of variegated silk, incense-burners and flower vases,

---

2. *A General Collection of Voyages and Discoveries, Made by the Portuguese and the Spaniards, during the Fifteenth and Sixteenth Centuries*, London: W. Richardson, J. Bew, T. Hookham, J. and T. Egerton, and C. Stalker, 1789, p. 10.

silks of many colours in lining and exterior, lamps and candles, with other gifts, in order to manifest the high honour of the [Lord] Buddha. May His light shine upon the donors.

What was kept in check within the Ming navy by the influence of the Confucian cultural ethos is precisely the conquering and evangelical mentality.

While Machiavelli and his followers in the eighteenth and nineteenth centuries were advocating their realist statecraft (understood as an inventory of ruthless foreign-policy tactics practised on behalf of the wealth and power of the princes), China was holding steadily to its idealistic, even naive, governing principle of self-restraint, 'the rule of virtue' or 'the rule of benevolence'. In Lin Zexu's Letter of Advice to Queen Victoria, he argued his case with typical Chinese cultural logic:

I have heard that the smoking of opium is very strictly forbidden by your country; that is because the harm caused by opium is clearly understood. Since it is not permitted to do harm to your own country, then even less should you let it be passed on to harm other countries – how much less to China. Of all that China exports to foreign countries, there is not a single thing which is not beneficial to people: they are of benefit when eaten, or of benefit when used, or of benefit when resold: all are beneficial. Is there a single article from China which has done any harm to foreign countries?[3]

Such moral deploring evoked ferocious parliamentary debate in Britain. Sidney Herbert responded to Lin's appeal by arguing that unless 'men are blinded by the faction they cannot shut their eyes to the fact that we are engaged in a war without just cause, that we are endeavouring to maintain a trade resting

---

3. Lan Yuchun 藍玉春, *Diplomatic History of China* 中國外交史, Taipei: Sanmin, 2007, 58-9.

upon unsound principles, and to justify proceedings which are a disgrace to the British flag.' Yet other members of the House of Commons mocked Lin's apparent unworldlines, suggesting that '[h]e had been naïve enough in his headlong way to proceed against the whole foreign community in Canton... The Chinese had never so tactless an official as Lin, who had made the British Cabinet the present of a perfect case.' And the result was a parliamentary vote of 271 to 262, which backed the use of military force against Qing China.

I am not suggesting here that cultural ideals and values can be understood as the sole motivation behind Chinese activities inside and outside its territory. However, one cannot overlook the fact that culture did come to play an important role in Chinese statecraft in terms of both rhetoric and practice. In Stephen Chan's essay, the behaviour of the descendants of Confucius in the Dark Continent is difficult for the West to understand because such emphases on friendship and brotherhood, on the unquestioned responsibility of a Great Nation, and on civilized behaviour with virtuous ethics have not been factors in the tradition of Western realist approaches to global politics. *Guanxi* diplomacy – five sets of binaries and reciprocations: emperor and subject; husband and wife; father and son; older and younger siblings; friend with friend – gives African siblings greater equality, and considerable time and space for reciprocation. An ancient civilization's sense of cultural superiority, and the claims of a worthier social order, demand not an immediate return in terms of economic profit or political interest, but a benign recognition of long-term loyalty and reciprocation, and the reputation of a harmonious celestial world-view. Moral statesmanship and the practice of self-restraint identify the Chinese principles of interest-free loans, non-conditional aid and non-interference in Africa discernible features of Confucian statecraft. Such a template again differs philosophically and pragmatically from the taken-for-granted realist approach of the West.

In his renowned book, Joseph Nye names culture, cultural values and foreign policy as the sources of soft power, by which a country may 'obtain the outcomes it wants in world politics because other countries – admiring its values, emulating its example, aspiring to its level of prosperity and openness – want to follow it'. When a country's culture includes universal values and its policies promote values and interests that others share, this increases the probability of its obtaining its desired outcomes through *attraction*.[4] In the Sino–African case, the conceptual realm of Western 'universal values' such as liberty, democracy and human rights has been replaced by the Confucian values of brotherhood, benevolence, virtuous rule, *guanxi*, harmony, loyalty and reciprocation. Such soft power is exercised by Chinese diplomats and entrepreneurs.

Yet culture, although it has an impact, does not determine political-economic activities and state diplomacy. Soft power still faces hard realities. The international community has pointed to the cynical aspects of Chinese activities in Africa, the most commonly mentioned being that (i) China is working to secure its access to African oil by means of direct economic investment, increasing trade relations and benign political leverage (as leader of the Third World and within the G77) on African countries; (ii) the Chinese policy of non-intervention is actually fostering and harbouring dictatorship in Africa and threatening African democracy; (iii) non-conditional aid and interest-free loans contradict long-term Western efforts for the promotion of good governance in Africa; (iv) Chinese power plants, industry and construction often neglect environmental standards and

---

4. Joseph S. Nye, *Soft Power: The Means to Success in World Politics*, New York: Public Affairs, 2004, pp. 5, 31.

cause severe ecological damage; (v) Chinese entrepreneurs insist on Chinese majority ownership, market monopoly and cheap labour; (vi) Chinese managers refuse to have dealings with their workers, and tend to resort to bullying and violence out of unmitigated racism; (vii) Chinese activities in Africa are a new form of hegemony or neocolonialism. And through the Beijing Consensus, Confucian ethos and Confucius Institutes, China is ideologically reinforcing its Chineseness and a new mode of diplomatic relations that is known in Africa as the China Model.[5] And, adding to the list, (viii) China's brotherly love does not seem to apply to its closest sibling, Taiwan, in Africa, as both have resorted to so-called dollar diplomacy to obstruct African countries' establishment of formal diplomatic relations with the other. For example, US$24 million worth of grants and interest-free loans to Tanzania and a US$3.6 million grant to Zambia were among the more notable features of Chinese premier Li Peng's visit to Africa in 2002.[6] Both countries had also been courted by Taiwan.

How do we treat what might appear to be inconsistencies in approach, or alternatively the operation of a different rationale or Confucian cultural ethos, informing Chinese activities in Africa? Rationalizing the contradictory logics of culture at work in the practical realm is a complex task, as the true motives behind the economic and diplomatic policies of the state are difficult to pin down. It is no surprise that, with more than 800,000 Chinese currently working, living and running businesses in Africa,[7] and over 800 small and medium-sized businesses in-

5. Lee Jehua 李澤華 and Zhao Xian 趙賢, 'The Western Condemnations to China's Activities in Africa and Our Strategic Advice' 西方對中國在非洲活動的指責、影響及我國的對策建議, *The Frontline of Thoughts* 思想戰線, vol. 35, no. 2, 2009, pp. 121-6.

6. Ian Taylor, 'Taiwan's Foreign Policy and Africa: The Limitations of Dollar Diplomacy', *Journal of Contemporary China*, vol. 11, no. 30, 2002, p. 134.

7. *New Africa*, March 2008.

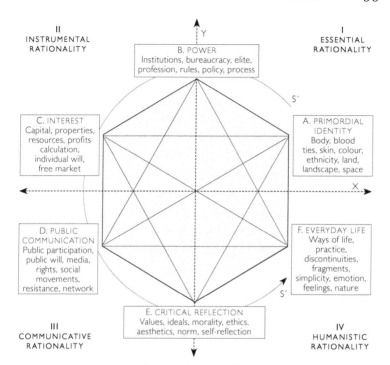

FIGURE 2.1 The logics of cultural governance

Source: Jerry C.Y. Liu, 'Discourses and Networks of Cultural Governance in Europe: A Critical Review', *Intergrams*, vol. 11, no. 2, 2011.

volved in manufacturing and in bidding for construction of ports, railways, hospitals, administrative buildings and other facilities, usually at a very competitive price, and benefiting from comparatively advantageous cheaper labour and other production factors, China today is perceived by many Western observers as a potential competitor or even threat.

In my view, critical reflection on cultural ideals, values, morality, ethics, aesthetics and norms (Figure 2.1, box E) is only one of the many 'rational' factors in human behaviour. There are also primordial elements such as blood ties, skin colour and land (box A); the workings of power, involving institutions, bureaucracy, elites, professions, rules and policy processes (box B); interests, including capital, property, resources, profit calculation and individual will (box C); public communications aspects, such as public participation, public will, media, rights, social movements, resistance, networks (box D); and the concerns of everyday life, taking in ways of living, practices, discontinuities, fragmentation, simplicity, emotions, feelings and nature (box F).

At the risk of gross oversimplification, we can observe that in the Western realist tradition an instrumental view of human reason, which emphasizes power, goal-orientation, profit and interest, and/or scientific and logical deduction and induction, seems to have the upper hand in deliberations involving global political economy. Weber even suggested that 'One of the most important aspect of the process of "rationalization" of action is the substitution for the unthinking acceptance of ancient custom, of deliberate adaptation to situations in terms of self-interest.'[8] The danger for the process of (instrumental) rationalization is, as Weber himself recognized, that it could proceed in a direction that would be at the expense not only of custom but also of emotional values and any belief in absolute values. This could lead to a tendency towards dehumanization.

However, in the Chinese case it seems that a more humanistic way of reasoning, which emphasizes moral-ethical cultural values and Confucian ideals, permeates traditional Chinese statecraft and governance and, as argued here, informs contemporary Sino–African relations. This mode of thinking places weight on the spirit of commonness in day-to-day life practices, on the self-generating moral-ethical senses of human beings, and on the spontaneous flow of human emotions. In the context of

---

8. Max Weber, *The Theory of Social and Economic Organisation*, trans. A.M. Henderson and Talcott Parsons, London: William Hodge, 1947, p. 112.

rational action, humanistic reason prioritizes not the calcula-
tive, scientific or logical articulation of interest for an individual
or a specific group, but a general and sympathetic understanding
of human desires, thinking and feelings as a whole.

I am not suggesting that Chinese politicians and entrepreneurs are idealistic and naive, or that Chinese activity in Africa
has nothing to do with addressing power, achieving goals, and
the calculation of profit and interest. I accept that the Confucian way of doing things in today's Africa is different from the
Confucian way in 1405 (Zheng He's expedition), 1650 (Emperor
Kongxi's Closed Door Policy), and 1843 (the Opium War), as
culture itself changes. And among Chinese actors and agents
in Africa today, there are politicians, diplomats, economists,
entrepreneurs, businessmen, scientists, technical engineers
and manual workers whose mode of thinking can vary from
one age and one individual to another. Chinese and Western
modes cannot simply be divided into two ideal types. Also many
Chinese are straightforwardly as pragmatic, profit-seeking and
power-hungry as Western realists.

So how and to what extent do philosophical rationale, Chineseness or – my term – 'cultural logics' affect, guide or express
Chinese officials' and entrepreneurs' attitudes, manners and
behaviour in Africa? If such cultural values do not actually 'determine' Chinese officials' and entrepreneurs' conduct in their
African strategy, what then is the function of such aspects of
cultural difference within the Confucian way? On this, Clifford
Geertz is certainly right in observing that 'One cannot run
symbolic forms through some sort of cultural assay to discover
their harmony content, their stability ratio, or their index of
incongruity.'[9] At most, one can only observe whether the forms

---

9. Clifford Geertz, *The Interpretation of Cultures*, New York: Basic Books, 1973, pp.
95-7.

in question are in fact coexisting, changing or interfering with one another in some way or other. However, values or beliefs (although they do not determine) induce in a person 'a certain distinctive set of dispositions (tendencies, capacities, propensities, skills, habits, liabilities), which lend a chronic character to the flow of his activity and the quality of his experience.' To us, such logics of culture represent 'a persisting tendency, a chronic inclination to perform certain sorts of acts and experience certain sorts of feeling in certain sorts of situations'.[10]

Culture matters. In the form of soft or diffused power, culture has returned to the terrain of international relations. And by bringing in new interpretations of a state's diplomatic strategies based on their embedded cultural norms and values, culture has rediscovered its place in the state's international strategy. For me, culture influences the practice of policymakers by permeating their ways of thinking and by containing them within certain value systems and cultural milieux, within which policy is determined in cultural debate rather than being the outcome of purely political-economic calculation. Such is the interplay of culture with hard power. In order to appeal to their colleagues and peoples, traditional and modern Chinese politicians would have had to negotiate within an overpowering Confucian cultural milieu. To put it another way, not only have Chinese officials often felt the need to justify adopting a pragmatic or utilitarian approach on moral grounds, or at least to interpret their pragmatism in morally and ethically compatible terms to win over the hearts of the people (domestic or abroad), but quite 'naturally' they would select a cultural explanation for their economic actions and political decisions. Cultural dicta permeate most official documentation. In failing to follow this

---

10. Ibid.

practice, politicians would expect to lose not only their political credibility, but also their personal integrity.[11]

It might be possible to envisage, then, a *reorientation* towards international cultural governance[12] along the lines of traditional Chinese cultural statecraft (the cosmopolitan perspective of *tienhsia*, the Confucian ethos of benevolence, virtuous rule, and non-aggressive Chinese internal/external relations), and soft power in Sino–African relations (non-intervention, non-conditional aid and interest-free loans)? That is, I suggest, we might be witnessing a 'cultural turn' or even an emerging 'paradigm shift' in global governance, the tendency of which is to shift the underlying logic of international governance from Machiavellian interest, wealth and power calculations to 'culture' - heralding a new mode of reasoning in state behaviour in the global political economy through debate on cultural values, moral-ethical ideals (with the challenge of brotherhood, benevolence, reciprocation and harmony) and a more balanced mode of human reasoning (i.e. a shift of rationality from quadrant II to that of quadrants III and IV in Figure 2.1).[13]

11. Jerry C.Y. Liu, 'Does Culture Matter? The Logics and Counter-logics of Culture in State Finance, Taxation and Tributary Trade Policies during the Ming Times *c.*1300-1600', *ICFAI Journal of History and Culture*, vol. 2, no. 1, 2008.

12. Andre Gunder Frank, *ReOrient: Global Economy in the Asian Age*, Berkeley, University of California Press, 1998.

13. Liu, 'Discourses and Networks of Cultural Governance in Europe'.

3

From revolution to business:
China's changing discourses on Africa

QING CAO

During his visit to Nigeria in July 2011, British prime minister David Cameron spoke about the problem of China's increasing 'authoritarian capitalism' in Africa and the value of 'liberal democracy' for Africa's future. The *Daily Mail* reported that 'Mr. Cameron admitted the West is increasingly alarmed by Beijing's leading role in the new "scramble for Africa".'[1] Chinese scholars react to such criticism with the charge of hypocrisy by invoking the iniquity of Western historical colonialism in Africa and the contemporary arrogance of imposing conditions on aid to and trade with Africa.[2] In step with Cameron, the US secretary of state Hillary Clinton, in her visit to Zambia in June 2011, warned African nations in Lusaka of the threat of 'neocolonialism' at the hands of external actors – implying China. Again, China was quick to point to America's much larger share of oil imports

1. 'Cameron Warns Africans over the "Chinese Invasion" as They Pour Billions into Continent', *Daily Mail*, 20 July 2011, www.dailymail.co.uk/news/article-2016677/Cameron-warns-Africans-Chinese-invasion-pour-billions-continent.html.
2. *Daodi shu xiang 'qinlue' feizhou* [Who Really Wants to Invade Africa?], *Global Times*, 2011, http://world.huanqiu.com/roll/2011-07/1851720.html.

from Africa and its undue paranoia concerning China's African engagement.[3] The backdrop to this recent discursive battle is the surge in China's business operations in Africa during the first decade of the new century. Trade between China and Africa grew from US$10 billion in 2000 to US$114.8 billion in 2010. China became Africa's largest trading partner in 2009.

Stephen Chan points rightly to the nature of Western alarmist reaction to China's role in Africa: it is Africa's resources that China is acquiring and that the West desires. David Cameron's mission in Africa was to boost business there, with twenty-five business leaders in his delegation; so was Hillary Clinton's in her trip to Lusaka. However, the African battleground is also political – China's 'no strings attached' aid and loans challenge the Western insistence on 'good governance' in offering similar deals. Intriguing is the fact that China and the West are both adamant that they are acting in the best interests of Africa. Undoubtedly entangled in the economic and political interests is the role of soft power being played out – winning the hearts and minds of the Dark Continent and the argument beyond it. Western popular imagery of Sino-African ventures is all too familiar – dealings between illiberal, authoritarian countries are fraught with corruption and exploitation. In the West's conceptual map, China and Africa belong to the same world of cultural 'other'; thus hard politics and economics are intertwined with soft assumptions and values. Different practices and presuppositions also produce curious contrasts. While 'African dictators' – Zimbabwe's Robert Mugabe, Sudan's Omar al-Bashir and Libya's Muammar Gaddafi – have been in the spotlight as villains holding Africa back in the Western media, African leaders (not

---

3. *Zai feizhou shixing xin zhimin zhuyi de maozi kou bu dao zhongguo de tou shang* [The Hat of Neo-colonialism in Africa Does Not Fit China], Xinhua News Agency, 2011. http://news.xinhuanet.com/world/201106/14/c_121535286.htm.

necessarily those 'villains') are portrayed in the Chinese media as official guests and agents of change in Sino–African cooperation. More intriguing is that Chinese stories about Africa do not reach the West any more than Western stories of Africa are told in China. These accounts are a monologue, not a dialogue – China and the West talk past each other, albeit with a common African audience in mind (likewise, genuine African voices are heard neither in the West nor in China). Yet stories are crucial in the modern era, as Joseph Nye has recently observed: 'traditionally, the mark of a great power was its ability to prevail in war. But in an information age, success depends not just on whose army wins but also on whose story wins.'[4] The differing rhetorics of China and the West reflect entrenched customs in terms of values, practices and visions of Africa and the evolving international order, despite their comparable business interests.

China's Africa discourse is underpinned by the foreign-policy priorities of different eras. Since 1949 the emphasis of African policies has followed a trajectory from ideological (Mao) to pragmatic (Deng) to business (current) interests, reflecting China's changing perception of the external world and domestic imperatives. Broadly speaking, four foreign-policy elements inform China's African discourse: (1) the 'three worlds' theory; (2) 'five principles of peaceful co-existence'; (3) 'peace and development'; and (4) the Chinese view of a new world order. These are also distinctive features of China's foreign relations.[5] Nevertheless a cultural perspective embedded in Confucianism provides the unifying link among these outlooks.

---

4. Joseph S. Nye, 'Power Shift', *Time*. 9 May 2011, p. 29,

5. Gerald Chan, *Chinese Perspectives on International Relations: A Framework of Analysis*, London: Macmillan, 1999.

The Confucian template

Stephen Chan sees much self-assurance in premier Zhou Enlai's masterly diplomatic manoeuvres with the West. Zhou's brilliance, however, belied China's predicament in international politics – Western containment, Soviet mischief and Asian suspicion in the depths of the Cold War. Africa offered a breathing space to Mao's China, with a financial cost China was always ready to accept, like a benevolent Confucian emperor. But the Chinese elites are painfully aware that the days of premier Zhuge Liang and his chivalry towards Meng Huo are long gone – the Middle Kingdom has seen itself besieged by external predators in modern times. China has suffered a deep sense of insecurity since the 'century of humiliation' (the Opium Wars started in 1840; the Japanese invasion ended in 1945), which contributed to an ingrained national psyche of victimhood that fuelled much of the twentieth-century radicalism. China was forced into the 'modern world' by Western gunboats, its sense of morality and universal order brutally violated. For over two millennia, China has grown used to a Sinocentric universal moral regime, with its own sense of justice, moral codes, patterns of behaviour, institutions and a language that encoded these assumptions and practices. Thus, unlike Japan, which readily embraced the metamorphosis into a 'modern nation' to ensure its survival, China agonizingly stumbled along the road to modernity from Qing emperors to PRC leaders. Despite post-Mao leaders' smooth talk of 'peace and development', China is still baffled by the confusion of the modern world, where it finds itself ill-equipped, inadequate and unable to adjust. China has dragged itself along in the 'modern' age for centuries, but its conceptual map – its fundamental world-view – has remained essentially unchanged. It simply does not have a lexicon that can engage effectively with the Western-dominated world where modernity-based rhetoric reigns, be it realpolitik, industrialism or liberal humanism.

Despite the facade of 'socialism with Chinese characteristics', Marxism has long lost its relevance since the reforms started in the late 1970s. Taking its place is the pragmatic developmentalism championed by Deng and his successors. The ritualistic respect accorded to Marxism derives from the political imperatives of the CCP's legitimacy and the need for some coherence with the recent revolutionary past. The Hu/Wen (President Hu Jintao and Premier Wen Jiabao) administration fell back on China's age-old traditions for inspiration. Indeed the PRC's political ideology, behaviour and organizational structure have been shaped heavily by China's traditions, notably Confucianism,[6] notwithstanding Maoism's iconoclastic attack on the latter. 'Going traditional' in international relations is part of the broader picture of 'de-Marxism' in post-reform China.[7] A Confucian imprint is visible in every step of China's engagement in Africa – from the brotherhood of anti-colonialism and anti-hegemonic Third World theory to the five principles of peaceful coexistence and co-prosperity developmentalism.

Moralism

The concept of 'soft power' is not new to the Chinese; for millennia China's scholar-officials preached and relied on the 'soft' appeal of Confucian benevolence to govern and bring unruly peripheral chieftains like Meng Huo within the Chinese orbit.[8]

---

6. Yongnian Zheng, *The Chinese Communist Party as Organisational Emperor: Culture, Representation and Transformation*, London and New York: Routledge, 2010.

7. Jisi Wang, 'International Relations Theory and the Study of Chinese Foreign Policy: A Chinese Perspective, in Thomas W. Robinson and David Shambaugh, eds, *Chinese Foreign Policy: Theory and Practice*, Oxford: Clarendon Press, 1994, pp.481–505.

8. Qing Cao, The Language of Soft Power: Mediating Socio-political Meanings in the Chinese Media, *Critical Arts: South–North Cultural and Media Studies*, vol. 25, no. 3, 2011, pp. 7–24.

Premier Zhu Geliang was unsatisfied with his clean military success until Meng Huo succumbed to the superiority of Confucian morality. China maintained its vast empire not by military occupation, but through a supreme sense of righteousness and the capacity to inculcate this in its tribute-bearing states. Chinese 'soft appeal' is thus different from Joseph Nye's notion of 'soft power' - designed as a complementary instrument to the supremacy of US hard power.[9] China's 'soft appeal' to Africa bears a Confucian hallmark - its primary objective is to win the moral argument. In Confucian parlance, this is *zheng min* - to have a recognized moral standing. In the absence of that, words are invalid (*yan bu shun*), which will lead to the failure of undertakings (*shi bu cheng*). Thus everything begins with and relies on the right moral standing being shared by all parties involved.

China's moral stance on Africa is subsumed under various discursive practices - not least its insistence on helping Africa as a true friend with aid and unconditional loans, and its perceived role as a champion of anti-colonialism. In China the idea of Africa, in both political discourse and popular consciousness, is associated with the image of victims of Western imperialism. For centuries, China's historiography has been imbued with a victimhood narrative centring on Western imperialist invasion and China's humiliation from the Opium Wars and the subsequent 'unequal treaties'. Mao's 'three worlds theory' and his enlisting of Asia, Africa and Latin America (*ya fei la*) in the 'Third World' camp are based on this shared historical legacy of being victims of Western colonialism. A moral leadership is assumed in Mao's dealings with Africa. As the Meng Huo story in Chan's essay demonstrates, the moral claim is held

---

9. Joseph S. Nye. *Soft Power: The Means to Success in World Politics*, New York: Public Affairs, 2004.

to be superior to political or military power, not because the Chinese do not seek political power but because traditionally China places a higher value on moral authority and believes that political power is the natural outcome of moral leadership. Moral status attracts political power, not vice versa, as the seasoned sinologist Lucian Pye explains.[10] Military means are considered a poor and inferior instrument by which to achieve political power; this is an unstable and unsustainable form of power such as tends to be acquired by morally corrupt rulers who have lost the 'mandate of Heaven'.

The international world system: political discourse

China has always emphasized political solidarity with Africa as a foundation for Sino–African relations in a sovereignty-centred discourse. By highlighting the shared anti-colonial tradition, China is asserting that it understands African views, feelings, conditions and problems. This 'natural tie' with 'African brothers' is at the forefront of China's Africa narrative, epitomized by China's policy on Africa: 'The long-standing Sino-African friendship has a firm foundation. China and Africa have similar historical sufferings. In their struggle for national liberation, they understood and supported each other and developed a deep friendship.'[11] The victim–brotherhood narrative has permeated Chinese leaders' speeches from Mao to Hu. Related to this is China's stress on the 'sanctity of sovereignty' for African nations, reflected in China's policy of non-interference and unconditional aid to Africa. China rejects a donor–recipient aid relationship,

10. Lucian Pye, *Asian Power and Authority*, Cambridge MA: Harvard University Press, 1985.

11. Xinhua News Agency, *Zhongguo dui feizhou zhengce wenjian* [China's Policy on Africa], Beijing: Xinhua News Agency, 2006. Full text available at: http://news.xinhuanet.com/politics/2006-01/12/content_4042317.htm.

claiming this would entail an unequal relationship and presume a position of superiority. Instead, China prefers the term 'partners': 'Sino–African partnership is essential to South–South cooperation, and has given it a new impetus. It helps enhance developing countries' status in the international politico-economic system, and plays an important role in promoting a just, rational, international politico-economic order.'[12] Despite its growing role in the global economy, China insists that it is a member of the Third World. However, the role of Africa in China's global diplomacy can be seen in Mao's often quoted metaphor: 'it is our African brothers who carried us into the United Nations'.

The road ahead

Recent years have seen notable changes in China's Africa discourse. First, key official documents have tended to feature reduced levels of political rhetoric, reflecting the transition from a political to a business-oriented relationship in the twenty-first century, and to some extent Western reactions to China's role in Africa. The 2010 *White Paper on Economic and Trade Cooperation between China and Africa*,[13] for instance, does not invoke any reference to victimhood in ties with Africa, as found in the 2006 *China's Policy on Africa*.[14] And it departs from the political character of the 2000 'Beijing Declaration of Sino–African Cooperation Forum'.[15] Second, China has reacted to criticisms arising in the past few years in Africa by issuing

---

12. State Council Information Office, *Zhongguo yu feizhou jingmao hezuo baipishu* [*White Paper on Economic and Trade Cooperation between China and Africa*], Beijing: State Council Information Office, 2010, http://politics.people.com.cn/GB/1026/13565932.html.

13. Ibid.

14. Xinhua News Agency, *Zhongguo dui feizhou zhengce wenjian*.

15. *Xinhua News Agency Zhongfei hezuo luntan Beijing xuanyan* [Beijing Declaration of Sino-African Cooperation Forum], Beijing: Xinhua News Agency, 2000, http://news.xinhuanet.com/ziliao/2003-11/24/content_1195597.htm.

new guidelines to resolve some of the highlighted problems. The 2010 *White Paper* details how China will handle a range of sensitive issues in Africa, including environmental protection, employing local workers, sustainable development of the local economy, employee welfare and corporate social responsibility. For the foreseeable future, China's foreign policy will continue to focus on fostering a favourable international environment for its economic development and seeking to expand external business activities – from obtaining resources to capital investment. To reduce tensions, China seeks new areas of cooperation with the USA, Europe and Japan – 'expanding and deepening our mutual interests and developing a fresh framework of interdependency' as one of China's chief strategists has put it.[16] China prides itself on granting Africa agency – that is, attaching no strings to aid and loans and giving Africans what they want rather than what China thinks Africa needs. The challenge, however, is to determine to whom such agency is conferred. China's dealings with some unsavoury African governments raise questions about who benefits most from China's aid and loans. *China's White Paper on Peaceful Development* asserts that China has broken from the traditional pattern that a rising power is bound to seek hegemony.[17] The 13,000-character White Paper aims to answer two fundamental questions that concern the West. The first is, what path of development has China chosen? The second is, what will China's development bring to the rest of the world? The ultimate test of China's world role in general and African engagement in particular is not what the West or China thinks or says, but what Africans (not just African governments) think and say about such a role and engagement; just as China should

---

16. Zheng, Bijian. *Zai lun zhongguo heping jueqi* [China's Peaceful Rise: Revisited], 2011, www.qstheory.cn/gj/zgwj/201105/t20110516_80784.htm.

17. State Council Information Office, *White Paper on China's Peaceful Development*, 2011, www.scio.gov.cn/zxbd/tt/jd/201109/t1000011.htm.

not worry too much about what the West says about the Chinese government, but rather listen to what people in China say. Joseph Nye is only half-right in claiming that the modern mark of power is who wins the story – for people live not in stories, but in real life.

4

Zhuge Liang and Meng Huo:
a metaphor for Sino–African relations?

L.H.M. LING

Stephen Chan refers in his essay to a famous episode from the fourteenth-century epic *Romance of the Three Kingdoms* (*Sanguo yanyi*). The epic centres on third-century Chinese politics and the specific episode in question is known, generally, as 'Seven Times Caught, Seven Times Released' (*qiqin qizong*). It refers to the decision of Zhuge Liang, prime minister of the Shu kingdom and renowned in Chinese history for his strategic acumen in war, to release Meng Huo, king of a Southern 'barbaric' tribe in what is today's Yunnan province, despite the latter's capture seven times. The prime minister lets the Southern king go free because Meng would not accept Shu rule 'in his heart' (*xin fu*) – until the seventh time. Caught alive, Meng is, as usual, accompanied by his wife and other relations. He enters the prime minister's tent in chains, only to find before him a fine meal of meats and wine. A soldier unshackles Meng and his group. One of Zhuge's trusted generals delivers this message to the King: 'The prime minister feels ashamed to meet you in person. He commands me to let you return home, to battle us another day. You may leave as soon as you like.'[1] The king is so moved that tears begin to flow. 'I may be a person outside of Chinese culture [*huawai zhi ren*]', the king weeps, 'but I still know what's right and proper [*liyi*]. How could I [alone] be [so] shameless [*xiouchi*]?' And, as legend tells us, Meng Huo finally accepts Shu rule.

Meng Huo, Chan writes, could serve as 'a metaphor for Africa'. By this, he means that Chinese history and culture have long treated the Other as a target of opportunity and reform, to be attained not through direct conquest per se, but through a strategy of patience to wear down the opposition.[2] Chinese superiority in terms of virtue and intelligence invariably wins. 'With great chivalry,' Chan writes, 'Zhuge sets Meng Huo free.' And Meng Huo falls for the ploy:

> On his seventh capture, Meng finally realizes he is being (consistently) defeated by someone who is not only superior militarily, but superior in virtue. When he realizes this, as in a sudden long-delayed revelation, he immediately capitulates.

Chan elaborates on the significance of this metaphor for Africa:

> China is prepared to work on Africa, despite any setbacks, for a very long time to come. This patience is reminiscent of Mao's favourite revolutionary ballet, *Taking Tiger Mountain by Strategy*. Sometimes frontal assault does not work. You can't just get it over and done with. Sometimes it's never quite done with. The televised epic I saw in Beijing never did have Meng Huo overcoming his taste in wine and concubines. Barbarians, even those adopted as younger brothers, never quite cease being barbarians.

---

1. *Sanguo Yanyi*, chapter 89, author's translation (http://cls.hs.yzu.edu.tw/san/bin/body.asp?CHNO=089; accessed 22 September 2011).
2. Called the *huairou* policy, it is translated as 'cherishing men from afar'. For an example of its application in the eighteenth-century, see James L. Hevia, *Cherishing Men from Afar: Qing Guest Ritual and the Macartney Embassy of 1793*, Durham NC: Duke University Press, 2002.

Chan seems sceptical, if not pessimistic, in this reading of the episode (dramatized in a television serial in 1994).[3] He suggests that neither China nor its perception of the Other changes despite intensive interactions with someone like Meng Huo. The Middle Kingdom retains a sense of 'superiority', if not 'virtue' then 'chivalry', towards Others. For this reason, African countries would do well to approach China with caution.

This episode deserves a fuller, more nuanced interpretation, I believe. And its implications for Sino–African relations could shift accordingly.

'Virtue' or 'chivalry' alone does not account for Zhuge Liang's actions regarding Meng Huo. Rather, a mix of Confucian, Daoist and Legalist philosophies, as well as the realpolitik of the day, frame the prime minister's world-view,[4] producing three specific principles: (1) target 'hearts and minds' as military strategy (*gong xin*); (2) draw on local talent as governing policy (*wei chen*); and (3) seek harmony as ethnic policy (*wei he*).[5] Capturing and releasing Meng Huo only begins the process. Zhuge furthers the other principles with subsequent actions. After Meng Huo accepts Shu rule, Zhuge Liang withdraws all his troops and puts in charge local men of talent and capability, including Meng Huo himself. (The 'barbaric' King later becomes a high-ranking official in the Shu court.[6]) Zhuge also orders his men to transfer important technical knowledge regarding agriculture and construction,

---

3. Interestingly, a remake of the epic in 2010, again in television serial form, omits this episode.

4. For an example of this world-view, see Ching-Chane Hwang and L.H.M. Ling, 'The Kitsch of War: Misappropriating Sun Tzu for an American Imperial Hypermasculinity', in Bina D'Costa and Katrina Lee-Koo, eds, *Gender and Global Politics in the Asia Pacific*, London: Palgrave Macmillan, 2009,. pp. 59–76.

5. Li Ming, 'Zhuge Liang 'qiqin meng huo' chuanshuode wenhua nei han chutan' [An Initial Examination of the Cultural Implications of Zhuge Liang's 'Seven Captures of Meng Huo'], *Lincang shifan gaodeng zhuanke xuexiao xuebao* [Journal of Lincang Teachers' College], vol. 17, no. 1, March 2008, pp. 7–10.

6. Ibid., p. 9.

salt and metals. In this way, he improves the material lives of the local people. Yet he leaves alone their customs and traditions, lifestyles and religions. The local people thus prosper on their own terms rather than those of the outsiders.

The epic underscores respect for the 'natives' in other ways as well. It includes a stirring passage on the martial arts and leadership of Meng Huo's queen, Madame Zhu Rong (*zhurong furen*). Three times she leads her troops to fight Zhuge's men. Three times they feign defeat (*zhabai*). She prudently refrains from chasing after them – until the third time. Seeing their retreat, she cannot resist and orders pursuit, only to find herself in a trap. Zhuge's men bring her to the prime minister. He orders her release in exchange for two generals whom Meng Huo has captured. The Southern king cannot refuse. And Zhuge Liang and Meng Huo enter another round of battle.

The epic closes this episode with Zhuge Liang's explanation for his actions:

> It would not be easy [*yi*] [to colonize the Southern tribes] for three reasons. Stationing outsiders would require a military occupation, but there is no way the troops could feed themselves [here], that's one difficulty. The barbaric peoples have suffered much, losing fathers and brothers [on the battlefield]. If I were to station outsiders here without troops, that would be a disaster in the making, that's a second difficulty. The barbaric peoples have murdered and killed, naturally they harbour suspicions, especially of outsiders, and that's a third difficulty. [For these reasons], I don't leave anyone behind and I don't transport away any supplies, [thereby] allowing us to remain in mutual peace and without incident [*wushi*].[7]

If only it were the case that George W. Bush had had such wisdom regarding Afghanistan and Iraq! The USA today would

---

7. *Sanguo Yanyi*, author's translation.

not then be saddled with two wars and two occupations in places unknown and far away, with multiple insurgencies daily sacrificing the blood and wealth of the masses for the interests and security of ruling elites. Whether Zhuge Liang actually achieves such a happy scenario in the South is subject to empirical, historical analysis – and not of concern here. For me, the significance of Zhuge Liang's approach to Meng Huo is its radical difference from the more familiar, Western model of colonial self-Other relations. Contra Zhuge Liang, Western colonialism appropriates both land and labour for the material benefit of the metropole at the expense of the colony,[8] while setting up a cultural and institutional hierarchy of race,[9] gender[10] and regime.[11] And if Others fail to 'comply' with conversion to this

8. See, for example, Walter Rodney, *How Europe Underdeveloped Africa*, London and Dar Es Salam: Bogle-L'Ouverture Publications, 1973; Timothy Mitchell, *Colonising Egypt*, Cambridge: Cambridge University Press, 1988; Arturo Escobar, *Encountering Development: The Making and Unmaking of the Third World*, Princeton NJ: Princeton University Press, 1995; Geeta Chowdhry and Sheila Nair, eds, *Power, Postcolonialism and International Relations: Reading Race, Gender and Class*, London: Routledge, 2002; Sankaran Krishna, *Globalisation and Postcolonialism*, Lanham MD: Rowman & Littlefield, 2008.

9. Japanese imperialism during the 1930s-1940s reinforced, rather than replaced, white imperialism, given the former's mimicry of the latter. To understand this phenomenon, we need to recognize the role of race, sex and gender in world politics. See L.H.M. Ling, 'Global Passions within Global Interests: Race, Gender, and Culture in Our Postcolonial Order', in Ronen Palan, ed., *Global Political Economy: Contemporary Theories*, London: Routledge, 2000, pp. 242-55; Robert Vitalis, 'Birth of a Discipline', in David Long and Brian C. Schmidt, eds, *Imperialism and Internationalism in the Discipline of International Relations*, Albany: State University of New York, 2005, pp. 159-82; Yumiko Mikanagi, *Masculinity and Japan's Foreign Relations*, Boulder CO: First Forum Press, 2011.

10. For a summary and critique of this literature, see Nancy Fraser, 'Feminism, Capitalism, and the Cunning of History', *New Left Review* 56, March/April 2009, pp. 97-117. See also Bina D'Costa and Katrina Lee-Koo, eds, *Gender and Global Politics in the Asia Pacific*, London: Palgrave Macmillan, 2009; Marianne Marchand and Anne Sisson Runyan, eds, *Gender and Global Restructuring: Sightings, Sites and Resistances*, London: Routledge, 2010.

11. Barry Buzan, 'China in International Society: Is "Peaceful Rise" Possible?', *Chinese Journal of International Politics* 3, 2010, pp. 5-36; G. John Ikenberry and Anne-Marie Slaughter, co-directors, *Forging a World of Liberty under Law: US National Security in the 21st Century*, Final Report of the Princeton Project on National Security, Princeton NJ: Woodrow Wilson School of Public and International Affairs, 2006, www.princeton.edu/~ppns/report.

'universal standard', then they are subject to 'discipline' from the 'international community'.[12]

Equally significant is Zhuge Liang's method. Although guided by Confucian principles, Zhuge nonetheless draws on the locality's specifics to develop appropriate strategies and policies. Appreciating the South's rich resources and understanding the fierce sense of independence of the local people, he aims not to crush the Other into submission but to win its *acceptance* – a very different basis for self–Other relations. From the fifteenth century onward, as the cost of acceptance, the West forced the Other's submission through slavery, gunboat diplomacy, military occupation and spiritual, if not intellectual, hegemony. For this reason, ruling elites in the West today worry deeply that a 'rising' China will not be 'responsible' – that is, abide by the international norms, rules and practices already in place.[13] This kind of rigidity sets the conditions for anger, alienation and ultimately physical violence, thereby perpetuating a cycle of terror that many mistake for world politics. 'Development' seeks to prevent, mitigate or unravel such violence. But without addressing the violent context in which development takes place, especially in terms of who gets to participate in making which decisions, we are left with fancy-sounding but ultimately empty slogans.[14]

Zhuge Liang, in short, thinks creatively. He does not simply apply a reductive logic whereby a general or universal principle

12. L.H.M. Ling, 'Neoliberal Neocolonialism: Comparing Enron with Asia's "Crony Capitalism"', in Dirk Wiemann, Agata Stopinska, Anke Bartels and Johannes Anger-müller, eds, *Discourses of Violence – Violence of Discourses: Critical Interventions, Transgressive Readings and Postnational Negotiations*, Frankfurt am Main: Peter Lang, 2005, pp. 93-105.

13. L.H.M. Ling, 'Beyond Westphalia: The "China Threat" Reframed', forthcoming.

14. See, for example, Alicia Yam and Sakiko Fukuda-Parr, 'Learning the Lessons of the MDGS: Second Time Round, Let's Get it Right', *Guardian*, 30 August 2011, www.guardian.co.uk/global-development/poverty-matters/2011/aug/30/millennium-development-goals-after-2015.

decides all. Nor does he focus only on the particulars. Rather, Zhuge draws together the universal with the particular, combining his own interests with those of the local people, and taking into consideration both the short-term and long-term consequences of his actions. Zhuge Liang thus develops a *sustainable* relationship with the Southern tribes, who honour him to this day.[15] Another famous episode highlights Zhuge Liang's ability to think outside the box. He fools the enemy into wasting much-needed arrows by sending a flotilla of grass- and straw-covered boats that appear to be on the verge of attack. The enemy reacts by shooting thousands of arrows into the boats, which are trapped intact in the grass and straw matting, and later retrieved by Zhuge's forces. In this way, Zhuge Liang not only deprives the enemy of precious arrows but also uses them, in turn, to restock his own arsenal.

The story of Zhuge Liang and Meng Huo conveys another kind of significance: the possibility of transformation in self–Other relations. From the start, Zhuge Liang aims not to eternalize his relationship with Meng Huo: 'I conqueror, you subject.' Rather, Zhuge seeks Meng's acceptance to eliminate conflict on the borders between their kingdoms by fostering a new sense of community between the Shu kingdom and Meng Huo's people. As mentioned, Meng Huo later becomes a high-ranking official in the Shu court. In both cases – the Shu court and Meng Huo, as well as his kingdom – evolve as a result. Here, it is important to note, the Chinese designation of Others as 'barbarian' (*man*) does not have the same fixity in role or meaning as that in the West.[16] *Man* indicates geographical and cultural distance from

---

15. Li Ming, 'Zhuge Liang 'qiqin meng huo' chuanshuode wenhua nei han chutan'.

16. For greater elaboration on the Chinese concept of 'barbarian' and its appropriation by the West, see Lydia H. Liu, *The Clash of Empires: The Invention of China in Modern World Making*, Cambridge MA: Harvard University Press, 2004.

the Confucian centre; but it is not an objectified condition.[17] Those whom Confucians label *man* do not lose their cultural integrity even though they are seen as beyond (Chinese) acculturation (*huawai*).

My own sense of pessimism/scepticism peaks at this point. That is, China itself may need acculturation. Today's China may be so immersed in Westphalian power politics that it feels the need to discard this older model of self-Other relations – or any alternative – to reproduce the West in the East to gain legitimacy. Current US-China relations provide an apt example. In response to Western portrayals of China as competitor, rival and possibly enemy, a muted presumption is affecting Chinese analysts and policymakers: 'they' (Americans/Westerners) don't understand 'us' (Chinese/China) – and 'they' never will. Yan Xuetong, Professor of International Relations and Dean of the Institute of International Studies at Tsinghua University, flatly states that the USA and China should give up the charade of a 'superficial friendship', constantly rocked by failed expectations and disappointments; he proposes instead a relationship of 'superficial enmity'.[18] This strategy would help to stabilize US-China relations, Yan asserts, since 'they have no way to become real friends' anyway.

Such binary thinking is taking hold among the younger generation. To affirm China's 'peaceful rise', Wang Bin advocates a policy of 'rational nationalism under patriotism' (*aiguozhuyi xiade lixingde minquizhuyi*).[19] This contrasts with the 'parochial

---

17. In this sense, Confucianism qualifies as a non-universalistic doctrine. See Zhang Xiangiong, 'The Philosophical Feature of Confucianism and its Position in Inter-Cultural Dialogue: Universalism or Non-Universalism?', *Frontiers in Philosophy from China*, vol. 4, no. 4, 2009, pp. 483–92.

18. 'Superficial enmity' entails 'preventative cooperation over mutually unfavourable interests and lowering mutual expectations of support, rather than ... adjusting concepts or improving mutual understanding.' Yan Xuetong, 'The Instability of China-US Relations', *Chinese Journal of International Politics* 3, 2010, pp. 263–92.

19. Wang Bin, *Zhongguo hepingjueqi yu minzhuzhuyi sichaode xingqi* [China's Peaceful

nationalism' (*xiaaide minzuzhuyi*) of old which indoctrinates the people with a 'superiority complex' (*yiouyue*), filling them with hate (*chouhen*). But nationalist anger remains unavoidable. It is simply 'infuriating' (*shizai rang ren fenmen*), notes Peng Zhen, for the West to peddle a 'China threat' thesis, just like it did with the 'yellow peril'; after all, history shows that only 'weak powers' are accused of 'hegemony', while 'great powers' are glorified and emulated.[20]

Zhuge Liang would no doubt observe that dousing fire with fire only produces more fire. Postcolonial studies fully detail how a former 'great power' like Britain threatened all it encountered, including its own – for instance, the Irish and the Scots, and the working class.[21] Why should this logic be less applicable to the Chinese state? As for 'rational nationalism', how does a state manage this without descending into mob rule, jingoism, and/or demonization? History amply shows nationalism running amok, especially at times of war or when it is imminent.[22] And what checking mechanisms are there to prevent 'superficial enmity' from sliding into 'real enmity'?

In short, I respectfully disagree with Stephen Chan. Africa – and the USA, for that matter – would do well to activate the Zhuge Liang in China. If only it were still possible.

Rise and the Ideological Trend of Nationalism Emergence], Master's thesis, Department of International Politics, School of Humanities and Social Sciences, Yanbian University, May 2010.

20. Peng Zhen, '*Zhongguo weixie lun*' – *yingxiang yu duice* [On the Compact and Countermeasures of 'China Threat' Theory], Master's Thesis, Department of International Relations, School of Philosophy, History, and Culture, Xiangtan University, May 2010, p. 28.

21. See, for example, Ashis Nandy, *The Intimate Enemy: The Psychology of Colonialism*, New Delhi: Oxford University Press, 1988.

22. See, for example, John W. Dower, *War without Mercy: Race and Power in the Pacific War*, New York: Pantheon Books, 1986.

5

Back to basics:
it could be anyone and, anyway,
it's all hard work

XIAOMING HUANG

As ever, Stephen Chan's essay is wide-ranging and yet immensely rich, scholarly while being profoundly personal. It touches on many issues of significance to readers across the disciplines: from philosophy to agency; from the Middle Kingdom to the outlands; from China and Africa to global architecture; from Africanists to Sinologists; from Kissinger to Zhou Enlai; from the Chinese approach to the Beijing Consensus. A book could be written on each of these issues. In this short chapter, I want to comment on the problem of 'philosophy and agency,' touched upon early in the essay, but seen to underlie the essay throughout. I also differentiate the Chinese in Africa – the huge number of private entrepreneurs – from China as an official actor in Africa.

The problem of philosophy and agency is twofold. First, regarding the issue of China in Africa, and the fanfare that has attended it of late, Chan observes that 'The Chinese are not accorded philosophical reasons for wanting to be in Africa', and, 'the Africans are accorded no agency of their own'. This begs a number of questions. Why do the Chinese need philosophical reasons to be in Africa? Perhaps what has been written and said so far about why China is in Africa is not entirely convincing? Or perhaps the debates are too 'ideological', in the sense of the word commonly used in public discourse? There must be something deep and more profound, one suspects, behind China's activities and enterprises in Africa.

As for Africa being in need of agency of its own, it is true that Africa has never possessed it in our times. There was the 'flash in the pan' of romantic idealism after the First and Second World Wars that thought it knew how the world should be organized. And it was believed that the decolonialization of the 1960s and 1970s dealt with the problem of agency (this turned out to be a prolonged process in itself, extending well into the early 1990s when South Africa elected its own president). Decolonialization was undoubtedly positive for the Africans. And yet, sixty years years on, we still speak of the problem of agency in Africa with profound concern.

The two problems of philosophy and agency are closely related in my view. Let me explain each in turn. There is no mystery about why China is, or, more precisely, why the Chinese are, in Africa. They are in Africa because there are opportunities there.

To be sure, it is not entirely unimaginable that the government in Beijing might have a vision for Africa and ministries for their operational strategies in the continent. But to perceive all Chinese activities in Africa as effects of the government's strategic vision would be testimony to the power of the imagination and perhaps point to the illusory presence of a developmental state. What we witness in China's behaviour today is international entrepreneurialism. When Heinrich Barth travelled to Africa in the nineteenth century, he was a traveller. Likewise, when Wang Xiaoer ended up doing construction work in Darfur, he was earning income on which to live, just like his ancestors in the nineteenth century in Singapore, Dunedin, San Francisco or Rio. He would not know whether the government in Beijing had a grand strategy in Africa. Nor would he care whether this has anything to do with Confucius's world-view. In one way, humankind remains the same hundreds of years on: people seek better conditions and opportunities to survive and have a better life. Except that today the international system – nation-states, boundaries and identities, national, ethnical, cultural, legal or otherwise, have made these perennial human interests and activities, such as those of Chinese in Africa, appear to be unusual. They appeared particularly striking once Beijing's control of activities across national boundaries started gradually easing. The world has changed and people have moved on, and they have moved to Africa.

Now let me dwell further on the proposition that the world has changed. Here is what I mean by 'the world has changed': (1) the worldwide deployment of resources for efficiency is not a natural impulse of capitalism, but a human necessity. If the pursuit of efficiency and wealth on a global scale has been framed and debated largely in accord with the principles of the nation-state system, it is very difficult to continue to do so today. Our interests and activities are global; challenges and solutions are global; our way of life and relations are global. (2) National and international institutions have been adapting to this profound reality. (3) Thinking and acting along regional/continental boundaries are neither the cause of the problems, nor a solution to them. They are simply much less irrelevant today. (4) This shaping of the new global structure is, of course, not of China's making, but China finds itself embodying a great deal of its dynamics; indeed one can argue that much of the change in the world has been due to the change in the nature of China itself.

So, when we talk of China, the state, in Africa, there is no mystery as to why it is there. But it is nevertheless a profound fact that China is in Africa today. This is not about China; it is about the world we live in. So the 'philosophical reasons' for China being in Africa, I suggest, are an expression of the profound changes shaping the world itself, of the same magnitude and significance as those brought on by the Industrial Revolution in Europe a few hundred years ago, or analogous to the reforms and restructuring of the Qin dynasty in East Asia a few thousand years ago.

Now let us consider the need for Africa to have agency of its own - that is, how Africa can control its own destiny and enjoy power, status and influence in the world. Africa has not achieved this so far for two reasons. First, the world is no longer defined solely by nation-states, and much less so by continents. Because we live in an increasingly interdependent and integrated world, no country can wholly control its own affairs - not the Americans, or the Chinese, and so one must ask why Africans should be expected to do so. Actions and capacities in today's world are defined largely by the flows of materials, production, capital and people across boundaries. The notion that Africans should have an 'agency of their own' is very much a territorial conception.

Second, there is always a moral appeal behind the call for justice and sympathy for Africa. We trace what Africa is today back to European colonial times, to the core-periphery capitalist world system, to the superpower puppet wars of the 1970s and 1980s. Africa has been a victim in and subjected by all of these dynamics. It is open to speculation whether China will be a new source of problems for Africa or exert and deploy its Chineseness to help establish a different world order in and for the continent.

Unfortunately, China is a problematic factor in each of these scenarios. Naturally, a new rising power will be expected to foster hopes of a new, kinder and gentler world order. The United States was such 'a rising power' in the early last century. The Soviet Union after World War I was another. China may bring some degree of that to the world as well, along with its growing power and influence, even though it is still not seen or treated as being at the core of the world of principal movers and shakers. Perhaps, on account of its successful governance on a tremendously large scale in remote ancient times, as well as the nature of the world order and civilizational arrangements under such governance, China is positioned to provide the world with an alternative way of organizing politics, economy and society. But will China's might be kinder and gentler towards Africa than that of its predecessors? I call this notion the *Wilsonian fantasy*. Africa might be more fairly treated. If it is lucky, it might gain a sense of agency in the new structure if it ever turns out to be a reality and if it lasts. But an agent is such only if it possesses a degree of wealth and the capacity to constitute the structure, and in that regard states are very different.

The issue is, of course, how the wealth and capacity are achieved, and therefore respect and status earned. This is perhaps what is at the core of the problem of agency. There should be no expectation that the international powers - the new rising or risen China included - will help. It is not something other countries can will, design or implement for another. This is not in the genes of the international system. Nor should international organizations be expected to assist; for we have seen what they can do for a country. Testimony to this is the continuation of Africa's lack of agency itself. Africa may receive aid from them, but this does not change things fundamentally.

Now here is how a philosophical China meets an agency-hungry Africa. What China means for Africa, in my view, is not so much Confucius, Bruce Lee or chopsticks. These may appear to be exotic and be good for cultural fusion. But they do not answer the real African challenge. What China means for Africa concerns not so much products, capital and resources either. These are universal rather than peculiarly Chinese. If it wasn't the Chinese, then someone else would fill the role. Indeed, the Europeans did so long while ago and indeed are still doing so. The Chinese are not be the first, and certainly will not be the last to be in Africa, as traders, travellers, settlers or anything else.

China's significance to Africa is in fact a very recent development – and it replicates what happened to China itself. The rise and expansion of the European powers and international society in early modern times created the problem of agency not only in Africa, but also in Latin America, North America, South Asia, Southeast Asia and, yes, East Asia. North America and Australasia were largely transformed from colonized to colonizer, thereby removing the problem of agency in these countries. Much of the colonization in the rest of the world was 'reversed' after World War II. For a country to be able to exercise its own agency requires more than just the removal of colonial agents.

Immanuel Wallerstein divides countries into two groups: Group A – those with wealth and capacity, which he calls 'core countries'; and Group B – those with little or no wealth or capacity, which he calls 'peripheral countries'. The world system is largely structured around these two groups of countries, according to Wallerstein. The problem with this world system is that the bifurcated structure is historically determined by the profound logic of the modern world economy – structure,

process, dynamics, as well the movement of materials, products, capital and people, in search of maximum efficiency in
production and effectiveness in capitalization on a global scale.
Such a system inevitably leads to concentrations of ownership,
productive capacity and purchasing power, and to differentia-
tions of role and function of each unit in the system. As the rich
get richer and the poor get poorer, so to speak, there exists an
insurmountable divide between the core and the peripheral
countries. Yet China's story over the past thirty years has plainly
demonstrated that this construct might be problematic. Thirty
years ago China was undoubtedly part of the periphery, but
it has clearly managed to move forward and indeed upward.
Today, no one would consider China to be still in the periphery.
China may not be at the top yet, but it has achieved more than
simply develop its own agency, by itself, and probably not in any
acclaimed 'Chinese' way.

This is the China story for Africa: you can do it; it is only
you that can do it; and you have to do what it takes. We have
heard a great deal about the China model. But the notion can be
misleading, especially after being worked up by well-intentioned
scholars and political commentators. It would be even worse if
the China model were to be conceived as an alternative means
to save the world. For the essence of the China model is that
China has not been guided by a model. China gave up long ago
on the idealist dreams of foreign thinkers determined to help it
become wealthy and strong, and ceased to call on its ancestors to
assist it in waving a cultural and spiritual magic wand to 'turn
iron into gold'. Wealth and capacity are the cumulative effects
of people's hard, effective, useful work and activity.

This is where I see the true meaningful connection between
China and Africa.

PART III

African outlooks

6

China and Africa:
an African view

PATRICK MAZIMHAKA

I write this as a response to the contributions of other authors
to this volume, from my recent experience as a senior official
within the African Union, and as someone who grew up in an
Africa where Chinese help was very visible and highly valued.
The youthful idealism of my generation was fed by the Chinese
example; it is not the case that, as some recent commentators
seem to think, China suddenly appeared in Africa. For these
reasons, I have approached my chapter in a different way from
that of fellow contributors to this second part of the collection.
I begin with a short account of history, and weave into it some
of my own personal history. It seems to me that no one asks
the question, how do Africans feel about China? That is, what
does China represent to them? To the contrary, the discourse
always seems to be one where Africa is being acted upon, or in
some way acted against. So in the first half of this essay I put
forward a different perspective. In the second half I comment
on the contributions of my Chinese colleagues to this volume,
but I also spend time discussing the Trilateral Dialogue, which

is in many ways a particularly important accomplishment in which Africans, Chinese and Americans sat as equal partners. The African contribution to this dialogue, which I helped lead, is a factor that becomes apparent later in the book. Not much has been written of the Trilateral Dialogue, even though it tried to restructure the underlying principles of debate over Africa in both Washington DC and Beijing. From my point of view it sought to restructure these principles on African terms. Stephen Chan sat and helped the African delegation at all three meetings of the Trilateral Dialogue, in Tswalu (South Africa), Beijing and Washington DC. Perhaps – and I hope Stephen does not raise an eyebrow here – this was an example of a form of Sino-African cooperation; though the African delegation was keen to advance its position as a case for Africa, mature and able in today's world, regardless of whether its partner was the USA or China.

China and Africa have had benign contact most likely since medieval times, but it is only in the last sixty years that political cooperation in the international arena, accompanied by Chinese aid, has occurred. This has been followed by serious trade and investment in the past twenty years. Political collaboration marked the decolonization and Cold War periods, which also saw the admission of Communist China to the United Nations with the support of newly independent African nations.

The contemporary apparent surge in economic engagement fits in well with the current political economy of both China and Africa, and Africa would do well to learn from China's rapid economic growth over the last thirty years in order to fashion its own development policies. This does not mean that the Chinese growth path should be mimicked by African countries, but there are lessons to be learned from it, as there are from the other successful economies of Asia and the Americas.

China-Africa cooperation today is on a good footing, as there is a strong coincidence of interests in the political and economic domains. Even if one assumes that the courtship has been mutual, China has been clearer about the path it wants this relationship to take. Africa, for its part, due to its nature - a grouping of sovereign states - lacks the necessary cohesion to respond to the challenge with the appropriate sense of urgency.

Precolonial contacts between China and Africa

It is generally accepted that precolonial Sino-Africa contacts were established as early as 700 CE and lasted until 1800. Large armadas visited the north, east and west coasts of the continent, making contact with Africans.

It is also true that the contact was generally benign, as Jerry Liu puts it when he compares Chinese to Portuguese contact with Africa, between 1400 and 1433. Whereas the Portuguese conquered and made off with both materials and slaves, the Chinese exchanged gifts. What he did not say, however, is that the Chinese took with them animal species (lions, rhinoceros, ostriches, giraffes etc.), alongside, probably, some African leaders.

Regular China-Africa contact dates back to medieval times, when all peoples of the Indian Ocean rim were freely sailing around and exchanging goods. There is abundant archeological evidence to support this.

China meets Africa in the era of liberation

In 1963 I met the first Rwandans to have returned from military training in China. I was a refugee in a camp in Uganda; around that time, several groups of nationalist guerrilla fighters in

Rwanda were attempting to overthrow the independence government that had been put in place in 1962 after a bloody referendum and a sham election, which were followed by the expulsion of the Tutsi, a minority group in the country. The group was related to or associated with the monarchs who ruled the kingdom of Rwanda before and during the colonial era. The expulsion was carried out with the assistance of the Belgian administration and, since Rwanda was a UN protectorate mandated to Belgium, the whole saga was duly observed by the United Nations. These events are widely considered as the first genocide of the Tutsi because mass killings and forced displacements took place during the process of expulsion. My encounter was not very different from the one that took place in Zimbabwe, as described by Stephen Chan, in terms of its surprise and shock value; but my reaction, upon meeting the Rwandan trainees in that refugee camp, was very different from his. The stories these shadowy warriors told of their experience with China, with its peoples and its complex culture, and of their newly acquired military skills left me and my young colleagues awestruck. I wanted to go to China, but I was only 14. As I grew older, my awe turned to intellectual curiosity. That is how I became an avid reader of the Little Red Book and other revolutionary writings by Mao Zedong.

China, through contacts with emerging African nationalist leaders like Abdel Gamal Nasser of Egypt and Kwame Nkrumah of Ghana, supported the decolonization struggles taking place in many African countries. Africans were trained in guerrilla warfare, imbued with Maoist ideology and guerrilla tactics, and they received arms and munitions with which to prosecute war. The trainees carried the Little Red Book everywhere and read it extensively, and mastered the use of the Chinese-manufactured AK-47. Young admirers of Mao Zedong like me read the Little

Red Book and much later Muammar Gaddafi's Green Book and helped distribute them both to street vendors at our peril. Inspired as we were by the new ideas contained therein, it was obvious that they sharply contrasted with the traditional Christian missionary education with which we grew up. Christian-based education prepared us to become righteous so that we might go to heaven – a notion of which place, where we knew that even the missionaries had never been, was difficult to grasp. We were, however, trained to serve colonial governments dutifully and unquestioningly; and to obey the kings and queens of their homelands. What we learnt from Mao, Gaddafi and others of their ilk was the urgent fundamental need for *liberation* of our country and our people from foreign domination. A liberation, we were told, was worth dying for if necessary. Besides, they would teach and train those who wanted to know how to go about joining this liberation movement, and they were willing to help with weapons to achieve liberation goals.

China's assistance in the decolonization wars covered Algeria, the Democratic Republic of the Congo (then Zaire), Mozambique, Zimbabwe, Angola, Sudan, Ethiopia and Eritrea, and Africans saw China as a viable source of all manner of weapons and moral support. China was actively engaged in promotion of its version of the Three Worlds Theory – which, as discussed by Chan, was developed by Mao Zedong, and later elaborated by Deng Xiaoping – in which the superpowers, the USA and the Soviet Union, formed the First World and their developed allies the Second. The Third World was basically the same in all definitions, consisting mainly of countries of the Non-Aligned Movement. The difference between China's Three Worlds Theory and that of the West was that the latter had the USA and its allies as the First World and the Soviet Union and its allies as the Second. The Third World was, as with China's version, composed of the non-aligned and the neutral countries. China may have helped African countries in furtherance of this ideological view, but the struggling Africans did not necessarily grasp the bigger picture, and focused instead on taking whatever help they could to redress a relationship with the colonial masters that had gone terribly sour. The participation of Africans in the Second World War - a war that took them to all African and Asian theatres - taught them that they, like their colonial masters, needed to live in dignity and that no price was too high to pay for attainment of this state.

In terms of approach, the Chinese did not use the big stick. They let Africans know that China was a poor country like theirs, a country that had been a target of Western, Soviet and Japanese imperialism but that survived because of its superior morality and its determination. They taught Confucianism and the Maoist revolution but not in the manner in which Christianity was introduced to Africa. Christian missionaries proselytized, gave rewards here on earth (jobs, better health, Western education) and promised life after death. Above all, they taught converts not to tolerate those among them, including members of their own families and communities, who had not accepted conversion to Christianity. China, on the other hand, adopted a much less heavy-handed approach, focusing on alignment with the emerging nations of the Third World on the basis of their needs rather than ideology.

From Chan's rendering of the Meng Huo metaphor one may understand the reluctance of the Chinese to impose or make adoption of Maoism a precondition for aid to the Africans, in the manner of the Western powers and the Soviet Union. Thus there never developed Maoist movements as there are in Asia; in all only one or two African regimes claimed to be Maoist. True Maoist enthusiasts were mainly young people who sold the Little

Red Book on street corners, only a very few of whom found their way to China for training in guerrilla warfare. Those political leaders who did subscribe to the Chinese view on the ordering of the world even went so far as to reject Western customs by adopting a version of the Mao Zedong cut of suit, with short sleeves and a round neck. Mwalimu Julius Nyerere in Tanzania and Kenneth Kaunda in Zambia led the political fashion revolution through their insistence on eschewing the Western suit and tie and opting instead for safari and Kaunda suits, and their example greatly popularized such clothing. These styles quickly became commonplace with politicians, locals and tourists alike. It is telling, however, that the Mao suit was adapted to produce an African version, which was thus never quite the same as the Chinese style. The rejection of total identification with this small but highly visible symbol of Maoism indicated a deep-rooted fear of communism, despite the fact that it was Chinese and therefore synonymous with liberation. Another way in which China failed to gain a strong footing in Africa in the colonial/postcolonial era was the fact that academic scholarships offered by China remained less popular than those offered by colonial masters, and much less popular than the massive student exchange programme inspired by President Kennedy's Peace Corps movement. President Kennedy was right in judging that the Peace Corps would help the USA penetrate the new Africa's policymaking class, which would otherwise remain dominated by the former colonial masters. Arguably China never managed to gain a foothold in the intellectual world of the Africans, many of whom it helped free from colonialism.

China, however, continued to endear itself to Africans with gifts such as sports stadiums, concessional loans and grants for infrastructure (roads, hydroelectric dams, irrigation schemes for paddy rice, etc.). In this and other ways it won African support for its admittance to the United Nations. The rapidly increasing number of new African nations being admitted to the UN certainly swung the vote in favour of China's admission to the world body. In addition, China needed to maintain its One China policy and it considered any attempt to recognize Taiwan as interference in its internal affairs and a very hostile act. This resonated well with African states, which had made respect for each other's sovereignty a key policy of the Organization of African Unity (OAU).

Capitalism, communism, China and Africa during the Cold War

Rumblings of independence started in Africa following the exposure of Africans to modern warfare and weaponry in the battlefields of North Africa and Asia. Two other important events that would shift the geopolitics of the time in favour of African independence were unfolding by the end of World War II. First, the USA and the Soviet Union, erstwhile allies against Nazi Germany, began a deadly game to control the rest of the world. The competition was one without open wars, except in Korea and Vietnam, conflicts which, if not proxy wars, were conducted sufficiently far from home for the rivalry to be dubbed nevertheless the Cold War. Second, China itself succumbed to a communist revolution in 1949, but it did not have the economic and technological capacity to compete with the newly self-appointed superpowers until many years later.

European colonialists regarded the call for independence as communist subversion inspired by the Soviet Union within the framework of the Cold War but, in panic, reacted by expediting independence, particularly of British colonies, starting with Ghana. As Martin Meredith wrote, 'when ... riots erupted in the Gold Coast, hitherto regarded as Britain's model colony, the governor, Sir Gerald Creasy, who had recently arrived from London, was quick to detect what he believed to be a communist conspiracy'.[1] This was after the Communist takeover of Prague, after which the West collectively took a stand against any further spread of Communism. Governor Creasy used a common strategic currency in referring to the events in the Gold Coast (Ghana) as a Communist takeover and as new forms of terrorism.

In many countries, the missionaries spread stories of the Communist monster among children in the church and in the schools they controlled. Christian families were threatened with excommunication should any member be associated with the independence movements, which were falsely and deliberately identified with Communism. School-age children were terrorized into rushing home after school for fear of meeting the Communist monster in the dark. Governor Creasy was not alone, however. Correspondence from colonial administrators and missionaries of the time is replete with such stories.

Newly independent countries were buffeted by the competing forces of capitalism and socialism, led by the USA and the Soviet Union respectively. Colonial masters – caught off guard by the rapid radicalization of the new ideological positions of their former subject nations, and by the ogre that Communism had become – set out to disorganize nationalist movements. Whereas the liberation leadership, like that of Kwame Nkrumah and Sékou Touré, felt the need to anchor their development models in an alternative framework and choose socialism, many of their deeply Christianized colleagues sought a middle ground and tried to soften the blows by flirting with the new third force: China. It is along these two paths, mutating through various

1. Martin Meredith, *The Fate of Africa: A History of Fifty Years of Independence*, London: Free Press, 2006, p. 13.

forms along the way, that Africa has been lurching forward like a rudderless ship for the past sixty years, while maintaining a unity of purpose for the total liberation of Africa. This did have a few exceptions, such as Côte d'Ivoire and Malawi, which continued flirting with apartheid South Africa to the bitter end, to the shame of their leaders of the time.

China made public its interest in Africa at the 1955 Bandung Conference, and from that time onward worked with African leaders to develop a powerful Third World lobby in international affairs. For example, when African leaders like Nkrumah and Nasser joined Tito (Yugoslavia), Nehru (India) and Sukarno (Indonesia) to form the Non-Aligned Movement (NAM) in 1961, China saw an opportunity and a tool with which to fend off its ideological arch-rivals, the Soviet Union and the pro-Taiwan West. China strongly identified with the views of this heterogeneous group, covering countries from Eastern Europe, the Caribbean, Central and Latin America, and most importantly Africa, on all international issues. Together they joined forces to push for decolonization, an effort to which China contributed resources, weapons, training, and funding for development. Mutual diplomatic support has been a constant feature of Sino–African relations since that time.

The ultimate gift

China has therefore long dispensed all manner of development aid and military assistance to African countries regardless of many differences, with the only caveat being African non-recognition of Taiwan. Until very recently, perhaps up to the last African Union Summit in January 2012, China tended to have dealings not with the African Union but with individual African states, through the China–Africa Cooperation Forum launched in 2000, to avoid fully embracing an organization that counted among its members countries which had diplomatic relations with Taiwan. It should be noted here that relations between Beijing and Taipei have recently been improving, particularly in terms of people-to-people contact.

With full cognizance of the extent to which the AU leadership has helped in whittling down support for Taiwan, China agreed to construct an extension to the African Union Headquarters, which opened during the January 2012 AU Summit, in Addis Ababa, Ethiopia. The building was requested by former African Union Commission chairperson, Alpha Oumar Konaré, a man of strong belief in Africa–China relations and a long-term personal friend of China. The building was designed through a nation-wide competition entered into by the most prestigious schools of architecture in China. The final design of the building was completed in cooperation with African Union staff and consult-ants and was endorsed by heads of state and government at their Summit in Accra, Ghana, in July 2007.

As the building was given to the African Union as a gift, the cost remains known only to the Chinese authorities. However, it is estimated to have cost approximately US$200 million. The land upon which the headquarters is situated was donated by the Ethiopian government and the city of Addis Ababa, just as Emperor Haile Selassie had donated land in 1963. The donation by the Ethiopian government was to pre-empt a decision favour-ing either Ghana or Egypt, because both had bid to host the new organization but no decision had yet been taken. The two countries lost the right to host the OAU as time passed and new contenders, notably Libya, joined the fray. After long and often acrimonious debate on the issue, the African Union formally adopted Addis Ababa, Ethiopia, as its headquarters and the decision was captured in the Constitutive Act adopted in 2000.

It was therefore correct for the government of Ethiopia to do all it could to have a fitting home constructed for the organization that gave the country the honour to host it – and it turned to China for help.

The government of China agreed to the request without hesitation. After a year of negotiation over the design, and legalizing the land acquisition, a ground-breaking ceremony was held in August 2008. The new AU headquarters building, which took three years to complete, was duly inaugurated at the end of January 2012.

The new building was indeed a gift to Africa, but what did it symbolize? Africa wanted it as a symbol of African unity. Ghana was quick to grab some of the honour when a statue of Kwame Nkrumah was erected at the entrance. Ethiopia and like-minded countries wanted it as a memorial to victims of human rights abuse in Africa, including those who perished under the Ethiopian military dictatorship (the Dergue) and other regimes in Africa, including victims of the genocide of the Tutsi in Rwanda, and others such as the Herero in Namibia. At the end of the day, it is seen as a memorial both to African hopes and tribulations and to Africa–China relations through thick and thin.

In the words of Jia Qinglin, a senior Chinese official who attended the inauguration, 'the building shows that China firmly commits itself to enhancing solidarity and cooperation with African countries, firmly supports African efforts for strength through unity and the integration process, and that China firmly supports a greater African role in international and regional affairs.'[2] In addition, Jia Qinglin outlined the following new policy elements in future China–Africa relations:

---

2. Jia Qinglin, 'Towards a Better Future with Stronger China–Africa Solidarity and Cooperation', speech delivered at the opening ceremony of the 18th African Union (AU) Summit, Addis Ababa, 29 January 2012.

- Promotion of friendship between China and Africa.
- Intensifying coordination and cooperation in international and regional issues.
- Endeavouring to raise the level of economic cooperation.
- Expanding people-to-people exchanges.
- Enhancing the development of the Forum on China–Africa Cooperation (FOCAC).[3]

China used the occasion to announce a gift of 600 million yuan ($95 million) over three years. Some of these funds are likely to be set aside for the maintenance of the new building.

All this generosity is premissed on reciprocity along the new policy lines outlined by the Chinese government, on the basis that the AU has become 'an important force for peace, stability and development in Africa' and that 'Africa will make even greater and more solid progress along the path of strength through UNITY'.[4]

The African leaders, and the African Union Commission leadership in particular, have to evaluate these strong signals and map out appropriate responses to these challenges. China does expect reciprocity.

How important is Africa to China?

Despite all the hype in academia and in Western and African media, Africa remains insignificant in China's trading relations with the world. A recent publication by the African Development Bank[5] shows that in comparison with the USA, Europe, Asia and Latin America, Africa is not a major trading partner with China.

3. Ibid.
4. Hu Jintao, speech at the inauguration of the building, Addis Ababa, January 2012.
5. *Chinese Trade and Investment Activities in Africa*, Addis Ababa: African Development Bank Group, 2011.

The sustained rapid growth of the Chinese economy, at over 9 per cent over the last thirty years, has increased the demand for energy and raw materials for which Africa remains a major source. The demand has also driven commodity prices consistently high, which is reflected in higher earnings for key producer countries such as Angola, Sudan, Zambia, Nigeria and South Africa.

Although China has increased trade (imports, exports, services and financial) with Africa, this is still limited to a few countries and a few commodities. Published figures show that China's trade with Africa has risen to US$122 billion in 2011[6] representing only 4 per cent of China's trade worldwide. For Africa this is 10 per cent of the continent's total trade. Foreign direct investment (FDI) totals US$5.4 billion.

China's trading interests remain largely in raw commodities such as oil (Sudan, Angola, Nigeria), minerals (DRC, Zambia, South Africa), timber (Equatorial Guinea and the Republic of the Congo). Chinese exports of manufactured goods go to a few countries that have had long-term relations with it – South Africa, Egypt, Nigeria and Morocco taking 60 per cent of the total.

China also competes with Africa on the world market, including in Africa, by providing cheaper processed goods. Lesotho and other countries lose out on textiles, South Africa and Mauritius on foods, Egypt and Algeria on refinery products, and Cameroon on timber products.

In order to retain a competitive position, Africa should shift its focus from low-technology industries to heavier ones such as automotive and aircraft manufacturing and maintenance, and the more lucrative IT sector. In addition, the cost of Chinese labour has been on the rise while that in Africa is now in decline in real terms.

---

6. Ibid.

China, however, has showed willingness to fund expansion of its trade relations by offering concessional loans and export credits through the China Exim Bank. Its aid programme has also expanded to cover most African countries, with the exception of those which maintain relations with Taiwan, only four at the last count (Swaziland, São Tomé e Príncipe, the Gambia and Burkina Faso).

China and the African Union

Through the Forum on China–Africa Cooperation, inaugurated in 2000, an expanding programme of cooperation at continental level is being achieved. China had been reluctant to deal with the African Union because its membership includes pro-Taiwan countries. At FOCAC each African head of state meets with the president of China individually; there is not a united voice at head-of-state level. The scope of the forum is set to be broadened in the next summit and more development funds and loans will be on the agenda.

China places great emphasis on symbols. As mentioned above, the latest is the gleaming new, recently opened African Union headquarters in Addis Ababa, Ethiopia. The officiating Chinese government representative, Jia Qinglin, called it 'the latest symbol of China-Africa friendship'.[7] In his message, President Hu Jintao set out current Chinese policy towards Africa, stating that FOCAC represents a new type of strategic partnership between China and Africa in all areas, 'making our political trust stronger, shared interests closer and friendship between our peoples deeper'.[8] The relationship among China, FOCAC and the African Union will be of great importance in the future.

7. Jia Qinglin, 'Towards a Better Future with Stronger China-Africa Solidarity and Cooperation', speech delivered at the opening ceremony of the 18th African Union Summit in Addis Ababa, 29 January 2012.

8. Hu Jintao, ibid.

The grand debate:
Africa–China–US Trilateral Dialogue

The rise of China–Africa trade has certainly provoked significant debate. In mid-2005 the Brenthurst Foundation in Johannesburg, led by Dr Greg Mills, sent a letter to Liu Guijin, then China's ambassador to South Africa, inviting China to participate in three-way talks involving also experts from Africa and the USA. It took Liu until the end of the year to secure agreement from Beijing. Thus it was that a unique set of discussions and negotiations took place in Tswali, South Africa, Beijung and Washington DC over a thirteen-month period: the Africa–China–USA Trilateral Dialogue.[9] I had the opportunity to participate in this process.

The nature of the Dialogue was unusual for the Chinese. It was to be a form of unofficial 'diplomacy', but involving people with an unusual degree of experience. On the US side, these were people who had enjoyed intimate access to and participated at the highest levels of diplomacy and foreign-policy formulation – and who still had access to their successors in office. They included: Andrew Young, former ambassador to the UN and member of the US cabinet; Thomas Pickering, former undersecretary of state for political affairs; Chester Crocker, former assistant secretary of state for Africa; David Goldwyn, former assistant secretary for energy; Witney Schneidman, former deputy assistant secretary of state for Africa; Nancy Soderberg, former ambassador to the UN; Princeton Lyman, former ambassador to South Africa; J. Stapleton Roy of Kissinger Associates and former ambassador to China.

---

9. *Africa–China–US Trilateral Dialogue*, Summary Report by the Brenthurst Foundation, Chinese Academy of Social Sciences, the Council on Foreign Relations, and Leon H. Sullivan Foundation, Johannesburg: Brenthurst Foundation, 2007.

The African delegation was a hybrid one: there were scholars and businessmen as well as counterparts to the Americans with diplomatic and foreign-policy experience, but it also included serving ministers – that is, members of the delegation held office at the time of the Dialogue. They included: Lopo do Nascimento, former prime minister of Angola; Sydney Mufamadi, minister of local and provincial government, South Africa; Neo Moroka, minister of commerce, Botswana; Greg Mills and Jonathan Oppenheimer of the Brenthurst Foundation, South Africa: HM King Letsie III of Lesotho; Joe Mollo, former high commissioner to the UK and ambassador to Canada, Lesotho; William Lyakurwa, director of the African Economic Research Consortium, Kenya; and myself.

In contrast, the Chinese delegation included no 'star' members from the world of diplomacy and foreign policy – although several senior former Chinese diplomats were among the observers at the Beijing session.

The structure of the Trilateral Dialogue was that each of the three 'sides' should be presented under the aegis of a recognized and prestigious non-governmental organization. The Brenthurst Foundation assembled the African delegation. In the USA, the Council on Foreign Relations, together with the Leon H. Sullivan Foundation, assembled the US delegation. In China, the partner institution was the Chinese Academy of Social Sciences – the leading think-tank in China. Although the leader of the Chinese delegation, Professor Yang Guang, director general of the Institute of West Asian and African Studies at the Chinese Academy of Social Sciences, held vice minister status, it seemed at first glance that the Chinese delegation was not as heavyweight as those from the USA and Africa. However, it turned out that several of the academicians on the delegation were advisers to the Politburo of the Chinese Communist Party.

Professor William Lyakurwa, executive director of the African Economic Research Consortium, was chair of the African delegation. Ambassador Princeton Lyman, formerly the first US ambassador to post-Apartheid South Africa, co-chaired the Americans on behalf of the Council on Foreign Relations; and Andrew Young, formerly US ambassador to the United Nations, co-chaired on behalf of the Leon H. Sullivan Foundation.

From a series of meetings, the African delegation to the Trilateral Dialogue prepared a paper entitled 'Competition or Partnership? China, United States, and Africa: An African View'. The authors discuss three key issues: development in Africa, Chinese interest in Africa, and whether there are areas of convergence among the interests of China, USA and Africa in this relationship. The conclusion, in brief, is that a 'win–win' strategy is possible. In the course of the meetings in the three continents, the participants came to the conclusion that in spite of differences in policies and methods of operation between China and the USA, there was no inherent strategic conflict between them over African resources; hence that cooperation between them is not only possible but is in the interest of all stakeholders.

This paper is reproduced in this volume, but it is worth noting a few points here. The paper was released at the Dialogue's last session, in Washington DC. This had originally been scheduled to take place in the White House itself but was moved at the last minute to accommodate security for the visit of General Petraeus, the US commander in Afghanistan. This illustrates the importance the Americans ascribed to the Dialogue. What was released in Washington was a series of papers, including the African one – which was put forward as a stand-alone paper. The African delegation had composed this paper at the previous meeting in Beijing, and it carefully draws upon comments made by members of the US delegation at the first meeting in Tswalu. There, Princeton Lyman had said that there is no strategic conflict between China and the USA over Africa. For instance, Lyman noted that China is very active in infrastructure, whereas the USA was absent from this sector. Lyman's remarks set the theme for the discussions at Tswalu, and were added to by Witney Schneidman, who argued that in fact there was a mutual interdependence among Africa, China and the USA in the African extractive sector. This was important for the African position, which was later drafted in Beijing and finally released in Washington. Basically, it was an African call for the continent of Africa to develop its own path, in full cooperation with others, but without conflict from others over the nature of the African path. In this way, all could win.

The African paper was designed to make an impression on US policymakers as an articulation of African independence, and to assert that Africa was not the victim of anyone, least of all the Chinese. Rhetorically at least, the Chinese in their pronouncements, for instance at the opening of the African Union Headquarters, mirror the African theme of independence and self-direction. That does not mean there are not problems with China, or that Africa has overcome or even begun to address properly all its development problems. It does mean, though, that Africa has made it clear that it values the freedom of choice in its partnerships.

China on key contentious issues in its dealings with Africa

Voices have been raised regarding China's 'sudden' appearance in the African marketplace. It is important to understand how China responds to this disquiet.

The first issue pertains to Africa's *development and global-ization*. China believes that African countries have not benefited equally from globalization and that 'it is the responsibility of the world community to help Africa develop, but at the same time, Africa must adapt to globalization'.[10] Africa should not look to China as simply the means to uplift its economy. The global market, including each domestic market, is extensive; it is up to African countries to create the conditions for competitiveness, reduce the cost of doing business, remove wage controls and avoid bottlenecks in the flow of goods. Other areas for improvement include institution building and legal reform, particularly in rela-tion to taxation, public markets and protection of investments.

The second issue concerns the principles of *non-interference in the internal affairs of other countries* and *good governance*. The West makes much of the fact that China does not impose conditions on aid on the basis of questionable governance. China has maintained that the first principle is a cornerstone of Chinese foreign policy, and the second a national issue. China contends that 'good governance' has no universal definition, even though the responsibility to protect, as upheld by the African Union and the United Nations, is a principle that is widely accepted. Democ-ratization should not be forced on Africa, as a people can develop under dictatorship. Nevertheless, as acknowledged earlier, it is in the long-term interest of Africa and China to liberate people and secure their endeavours with sound democratic governance.

Africa, through the African Union and its Commission, must therefore continue to develop norms for the protection of funda-mental rights, including of women, children and minorities, and to subject these to outside debate. The norms of good governance, including regular elections, are now generally accepted; and

---

10. *Africa–China–US Trilateral Dialogue*, Final Statement, Summary Report, p. 6.

China should have no problems with these if they are all-Africa-driven and not imposed from outside.

Africa's development situation

After fifty years of wandering in the uncertain wilderness of complex decolonization, the not-so-cold Cold War, Africa found a compass to help the continent navigate into the future. The adoption of the African Union Constitutive Act and the New Partnership for Africa's Development (NEPAD) signalled the beginning of a new era in the continent's politics, characterized by a search for unity of action on issues of importance to the continent, and the desire to seek principled strategic partnerships with the rest of the world.

Africa today enjoys privileged relations with China and the USA, with the European Union and its member states, with Japan and India, with Latin America and the Caribbean, and even with Turkey and Iran. Many of these countries have ambassadors exclusively accredited to the African Union. It is reasonable to assume that this level of representation implies higher levels of cooperation and reflects the strategic importance the parties see in each other.

Africa's development goals, broad as they are, will need all the support they can get, particularly from developed nations and emerging economies. Africa requires new and innovative technologies to create jobs, to be competitive, and to access the global market. Africa will have to demand fair prices for the raw materials needed by other economies. Africa can also learn from its partners' principles and tenets of sound economic management, such as transparent procurement procedures, clear taxation laws, fiscal responsibility in the public domain, and fair arbitration procedures.

In addition, Africa will need access to money markets, and to development funds designated for nationally determined development programmes. Aid does not seem to have a place in the longer-term scheme of things, since it has been found to be inimical to and tends to stunt local initiative. This has been widely recognized in the area of food and nutrition aid, where assisted families tend to be reluctant to return to farming as long as food aid remains available. Aid without the participation of beneficiaries diminishes individual responsibility. It is important to note that economic cooperation between Africa and its partners is not a one-way street. It is of mutual benefit and each party has a responsibility to nurture it for the common good. Africa will continue to pursue a growth path based on sourcing investment funds from money markets and from development aid for the foreseeable future. Africa needs to reach double-digit growth to start lifting itself out of the mire, and to do so it will need properly targeted funds. To achieve this, however, African leaders must acknowledge the past failures that marked what some call 'the lost decades', and make the right policy choices. Greg Mills, in his outstanding book *Why Africa is Poor and What Africans Can Do About It*,[11] states that 'The main reason Africa's people are poor is that their leaders have made this choice.' This may sound harsh, but the developing world is full of examples of sound policy decisions that have yielded spectacular results in our own time. China, with its steady growth over the last thirty years, is one of them. Singapore, South Korea, Vietnam and Costa Rica, to mention just a few, have turned their economies around with home-grown innovative policies. On the other hand, thirty years ago Côte d'Ivoire and Zimbabwe were the most developed

---

11. Johannesburg: Penguin, 2010.

economies in Africa, excepting South Africa and the North African countries, but they have recently been teetering on the verge of collapse.

Chinese interests in Africa

China's interests in Africa have historically been the same as those of other nations: driven by the search for knowledge and wealth. Whether this was profitable to Africa or not depends on the balance sheet one draws up for each period. However, more recently, including the period of African decolonization, China arguably had an interest in developing connections with Africa as part of its quest for a role in international relations: first, as an aggrieved party trying to gain access to the newly created United Nations organization; and second, as an ideological alternative to Western capitalism and imperialism and Soviet Communism. Africa and other emerging nations proved to be attractive allies through the Non-Aligned Movement and others in advancement of the Three Worlds Theory. China has always professed to be a poor country which cannot base its relations on a rich–poor dichotomy, but must live with its friends in reciprocation in true Confucian spirit – the spirit that is the subject of several contributions from Chinese colleagues in this volume. It is up Africa to figure out how to benefit from this relationship in the long term.

How do ordinary Africans
view the China–Africa relationship?

Today, many resource-rich African countries view China as an exploiter of their resources. In Zambia, for example, the issue dominated a recent presidential campaign. In Malawi, which has no major resources, a man of the cloth whom I should trust challenged me to explain why China had built a private house for the president, conveniently omitting to mention other investments in public infrastructure. African media and Africa-accessed media are replete with such stories. The inauguration of the African Union Headquarters in Ethiopia unleashed severe criticism, particularly in the electronic media, not only for what the authors termed 'the highly developed begging skills of African leaders', but also for the fact that the building was erected using Chinese labour.

More importantly, one should ask whether the ordinary African is happy with the gifts, loans and trade. Complaints include the use of Chinese labour, the treatment of locals by Chinese employers in mining and infrastructure projects, the deliberate social isolation of Chinese workers from the communities in which they live and work, the poor quality of Chinese goods, and the occasional infringement of customs and fiscal laws by individuals and companies.

Such animosity directed towards the 'Other', however, is commonplace; neither the Chinese nor their African hosts and beneficiaries should be unnecessarily alarmed, because such complaints are common both in Africa and elsewhere. Having lived and worked in foreign countries, within and outside the continent, I am aware that foreigners are bound to provoke unwarranted animosity in the locals. For example, South Africa fell into deep disgrace because of the way Zimbabwean economic migrants and refugees in the 2000s, in common with other foreigners, were routinely maltreated. Similarly, at the beginning of the 1980s, Nigeria expelled Africans from Ghana, Niger, Mali, Chad, Cameroon and Upper Volta (Burkina Faso), blaming them for ills engendered by the mismanagement of the ruling military elite. Thirty years later, Nigeria has once again expelled Africans from Niger, Chad and Mali, blaming them for its failure to deal with Islamic fundamentalists linked to al-Qaeda.

At the same time one notices the widespread lack of information available to Africa's citizenry on the amounts of funding China gives or loans to African countries. The problem is that African governments are unwilling or do not know how to inform their people so they are able to see misdemeanours in context. China's interests in Africa and those of Africa in China are converging – that is, to quote the phrase used by African participants in the Trilateral Dialogue, China–Africa relations increasingly have 'points of intersection or a coincidence of interests'.

China sidesteps ideology to move centre stage

The Chinese Communist Party has outdone itself in steering China towards a capitalist economy, through a series of reforms, without letting the Party militants get alarmed. China has steadfastly shunned the Christian underpinnings of Western capitalism, such as individual liberties, freedom of worship and of association in general, and has emphasized the preponderant role of the state in steering the development effort. What this means is that China, though ready and sometimes eager to aid Africa, particularly if it is in the interests of the Chinese state, will equally compete with African manufacturers in the African market. Textiles are an often cited example of this competition but, as mentioned earlier, there are other areas or industries that can be developed, perhaps in partnership, to mutual benefit.

China has been investing in Africa in long-term projects in the mineral and oil sectors; this will inevitably translate into a desire for improved governance in order to guarantee security for these investments. China has made 'non-interference in domestic affairs' a cornerstone of its foreign policy, although the recent engagements of its military and navy in Sudan and Somalia at the behest of the African Union seem to point to a different way in the future. China will soon have reason to insist on acceptable levels of accountability or what Western governments call 'acceptable good governance', commensurate with levels of investment. Of course these will not be any different from standards set by the West for Egypt, Angola, the Democratic Republic of the Congo or Equatorial Guinea, where expedience can dictate what is acceptable and what is not.

China will not promote democracy in Africa, or in China for that matter. African leaders, including those starry-eyed revolutionaries, have abandoned the democratic ideals of their youth and now flaunt World Bank 'Doing Business' indices and Mo Ibrahim reports, all based upon an unlikely macroeconomic stability, or malaria eradication and control of HIV rates, funded by the Global Fund or Bill and Melinda Gates, as indicators of good governance. Tunisia easily got to the top of the heap in this contest. The flouting of due process, constitutional rule and fundamental liberties is what will, in the end, undermine autocratic regimes and put at risk foreign, including Chinese, investment. So, as the African participants in the Trilateral Dialogue put it, 'promotion of democracy is also in the investors' enlightened self-interest' and in the interest of African citizens.

In his keynote essay in this volume, 'The Middle Kingdom and the Dark Continent: An Essay on China, Africa and Many Fault Lines', Stephen Chan reviews the historical relationship between China and Africa, the Chinese view of the 'Other', and the Confucian influence on how China deals with Africa, 'with compassion, moderation and humility'. Confucianism advocates generosity accompanied by reciprocation. He warns, however, that Africa should be cautious, and avoid romanticizing historical relations, in dealing with China. He believes China's trade with Africa will depend on favourable terms, political support and the availability of strategic commodities which China needs in order to compete with the rest of the world, including Africa itself, as mentioned earlier. Due to its rapid economic growth over the last thirty years, China has enough cash with which to secure commodities, and to reward those African countries which are prepared to reverse policy and accept the One China doctrine and, if necessary, protect China when it is attacked on its human rights record.

An example of reward for good behaviour is the case of Malawi, which had maintained diplomatic and economic relations with Taiwan since Hastings Kamuzu Banda's era, but then turned around in 2007 and broke relations with Taipei. It consequently benefited from a $260 million concessionary loan, and China–Malawi trade has risen to $100 million, representing a hefty 45 per cent of overall trade. A brand new parliament was built ($41 million) and a five-star hotel ($90 million) is under construction. This is just one instance of many that show that Chinese largesse is strategic and not romantic. China expects to be rewarded for its investment, in kind (politics and diplomacy) or in cash (profit for its businesses).

In accordance with Confucian patience, China will take more risk in its long-term lending to Africa than would the West, in spite of the complications that can arise. It is also the case that whenever the state or other national institutions, such as trade unions, raise complaints – as happened in Zambia, for example – the Chinese management has dealt with them promptly. It is also true that it is not only Chinese companies that abuse or underpay workers – both local and other international companies do so as well.

China–Africa and the fault lines

Stephen Chan's essay is most informative, and for some very provocative, but I consider its main strength to be its readability for those, like me, without expertise in Chinese traditional thought. I will not comment on the whole essay and its frame of reference because this has been done so capably by the volume's other authors. I will instead concentrate on the Chinese essays, where engagement with an Africa-influenced view may be productive.

Chan's observation that Africa comprises a number of complex countries has seemingly escaped Africans themselves, even though the failure to advance the notion of 'one Africa' as a centrally managed agglomeration, deriving benefits from the continent's abundant synergies, is evident for all to see. The rest of the world, however, has come to recognize the merits of dealing with an Africa which speaks with one voice on issues of importance. In the last decade, since the launch of the African Union, important players on the world stage, such as the USA, China, the European Union and the United Nations, have forged bilateral relations with the AU. Emerging economies such as Brazil, India, Turkey, and other countries such as Canada, Cuba and Mexico have diplomatic representation at the AU. These relationships translate into substantive support for Africa's programmes, including peacekeeping operations.

Newly independent African states had agreed to form the Organization of African Unity in 1963 with the unique remit of achieving full decolonization of the continent, including dismantling of the apartheid regime in South Africa, and of setting up a union of all African independent states. However, African leaders failed to agree on how to set about achieving these two objectives and on who would be their strategic partner, the West or the Soviet Union. This divide still haunts Africa, as was so painfully demonstrated during the 2007 African Union debate dedicated to the issue, held in Accra to mark the fiftieth anniversary of Ghana's independence. The debate evoked the spirit of 1963, with pan-African 'unionists' pitted against 'integrationists' and 'progressives' against 'conservatives'.

China, like any other nation, looks everywhere for the means to develop its economy, invest its wealth, and exert influence proportionate to that wealth. Africans need to understand that the Chinese approach, just like that of the West, is driven by materialism. Nevertheless, when listening to Chinese officials and indeed certain scholars, such as Jerry Liu in this volume, as an African I feel it is important to pay close attention to their language. We need to do so in order not to be deceived by the apparent or real difference between statecraft based on Confucian ethics and that based on Christian ethics. This need underpins the trilateral process referred to above.

In response to Chan, Lily Ling disagrees on the interpretation of the metaphor of Zhuge Liang, which according to Chan demonstrates Confucian ethics at play, the tenets of governance involving patience, virtue and generosity. Ling believes that rather than China discarding its Confucian 'self–Other relations', and maintaining that the younger generation is attracted by this binary thinking and perceives it as integral to China's peaceful rise, Zhuge's thought should be practised first in China. This is interesting because the Zhuge metaphor depicts the Other as a barbarian beyond immediate conversion; and yet at the same time she sees the need for China to open up to barbarian civilizing influences. Talking to a friend, a Rwandan Belgian who spent ten years as an expatriate in China teaching young Chinese, I asked if this meant that the Chinese were racist. His immediate answer was in the negative. He said that the Chinese have a highly developed sense of superiority over others – those whom some, including Chan, call the people of the periphery – but the difference is not expressed in terms of race. Arguably, what Lily Ling proposes in terms of domestic change may already be happening on account of the Chinese Internet and other global media.

The problematic issue of African agency that Chan raises is also commented on by Xiaoming Huang, who, in reference to the Zheng He adventures, observes that Africa has not had agency in the past but needs it now. Yet Africa compares well with other continents in terms of developing states and empires. It is widely recorded that 'by AD 1200, the process of civilization was reaching global dimensions. At the same time that Europe, Asia and the Middle East (including North Africa) were experiencing dynamic cultural growth during the medieval period, sub-Saharan Africa and the New World were undergoing similar changes. All areas had flourishing agriculture supported by expanding populations, large cities, highly skilled craftsmen, expanding trade, complex social order, and development.'[12] Before Zheng and the Portuguese crossed paths on the African shores, around 1400 CE, many African states existed and had agency.

These states could not have been developed and protected without the requisite wealth. In fact Africa, like China, lost its agency on account of superior technology ushered in by the Industrial Revolution in major European countries. Indeed the struggle for independence shows that when Africans were able to lay their hands on the same weapons as the colonizing powers, their priority was to restore the lost agency. But, as Huang notes, sixty years later Africa has still not fully found it, while China is

---

12. See 'Africa: Emerging Civilizations in Sub-Saharan Africa', www.historyworld.org/Africa.htm.

beginning to assert itself, due to its rapid economic development over the last thirty years.

Chan pertinently draws attention to the fault lines that might undermine China–Africa relations, and here few comments are needed. The first fault line he identifies is the fact that Africa is not the most important area of interest for China. And he is correct. But it would seem that China nevertheless still values its political relationship with Africa, even though this may seem romantic to some. After all, Africa has always stood by China in its hour of need, and this I believe has value. Examples of such loyalty include Tienanmen Square and the threat of sanctions; incessant resolutions in the UN Human Rights Commission concerning Taiwan and Tibet.

Chan's fifth, sixth, seventh and eighth fault lines probably show that China is willing to go a long way with Africa, although in reality the exposure is still very minimal. Lending against commodities is still safe even with a change of governance. Nowhere was this demonstrated better than in Zambia, where in spite of Michael Sata's earlier rhetoric and campaign threats against Chinese interests, nothing really happened when he became president; in fact he backtracked. Similarly, China recognized the need to develop relations with South Sudan before it split from the North. That was a well-thought-out strategic move with an almost instant positive result, for both North and South Sudan and for China.

Conclusion

The debate that is engaged through this process, and by Stephen Chan's wish to seek out views from China and Africa, is both welcome and, most importantly, timely. It is to be hoped that the debate will pick up momentum and more people will become involved.

Chan delineates what he considers the most 'mappable' fault lines. I will venture to add a couple, on the Africa side, that could in due course jeopardize the projected gains from the China–Africa relationship.

First, Africa has postponed the attainment of a union for far too long and for this reason is unable to take full advantage of its diverse geography, natural resources and demography. This diminishes Africa's bargaining power in the marketplace, where invariably the adage that united we stand and divided we fall fully plays out. Nkrumah, who has been restored to glory in the bronze statue at the new African Union building after fifty years of vilification, had called on Africans to seek the political kingdom first, meaning a political union of the continent. He was cut down. Hu Jintao echoed this call in his message to the gathered African heads of state and government and their friends when he said: 'We have every reason to believe that, under its [AU] guidance, Africa will make even greater and more solid progress along the path of *strength through unity*.' I hope that whenever our leaders pass by the imposing statue of Nkrumah to enter the splendid Plenary Hall, they will hear voices from the past – Nkrumah, Gaddafi and others – and from the present – Hu Jintao – and see the future of Africa more clearly.

Second, African states are vulnerable to violent changes of regime, and as such our investment ratings are very poor. African governance is so lacking that even the private sector seeking partnerships always looks for government guarantees for their investments. Good-governance reforms are often imposed on unwilling or reluctant leaders, who manipulate everything from economic data to census and election results to thwart efforts at reform. Such leaders cannot reassure investors or guarantee anything.

Relations with China are crucial for Africa. I hope our leaders will catch the fast-moving economic train that China has become for the benefit of their people. Today an opportunity exists for win-win economic cooperation and Africa must seize it.

7

Competition or partnership? China, the United States and Africa – an African view

LOPO DO NASCIMENTO, WILLIAM LYAKURWA,
PATRICK MAZIMHAKA, GREG MILLS, JOE MOLLO,
SYDNEY MUFAMADI & MICHAEL SPICER

China's rising profile in Africa is perhaps the most significant development for the continent since the end of the Cold War. It has sparked new interest in Africa's economic potential. It has helped to elevate interest in Africa in global affairs, a profile already raised by the continent's current economic growth spurt and homespun efforts to deal with conflict and institutionalize governance regimes. Finally, China's involvement has ended European and American complacency that Africa would always belong to their sphere of influence.

No other major power shows the same interest in Africa. The Forum on China–Africa Co-operation in November 2006, which included nearly every African head of state, was the largest diplomatic meeting in the history of the People's Republic. President Hu Jintao's February 2007 trip to Africa was a catalyst for all manner of speculation on China's role on the continent. Hu's recent trip – his fifth since 1999 and second in nine months – took him through eight African states in twelve days. It came on the heels of the visit by Chinese Premier Wen Jiabao to seven resource-rich African countries in June 2006, his third trip to the continent. Compare that record to the only two official trips made to Africa by a US president: Clinton in March 1998 and Bush five years later.

Does Beijing's extraordinary level of interest reflect Africa and China's economic maturity, or does it represent something sinister, a fresh attempt to exploit Africa's natural resources? Is it of benefit to Africa? And how will growing competition between China and the United States and European countries over Africa's natural resources turn out?

China's fresh involvement comes at a dynamic juncture in Africa's history. After years of being viewed as the 'hopeless continent', Africa is 'in play'. The continent may receive new aid (as high as $50 billion annually), and new investment flows, especially in the energy sector (potentially $40 billion over the next 15 years). But critical obstacles remain for the continent: principally, the twin challenges of lifting its 800 million people out of poverty, and of enjoying the technological fruits of globalization alongside increased capital and trade flows.

This paper identifies where there is a convergence and divergence between Africa's interests and those of the great powers and addresses what Africa might be able to do to ensure today's heightened activity on the continent is to its own advantage.[1]

Africa's development situation

In Africa, the fifty years since the independence of Ghana in March 1957 were dominated by the 'great' issues of

1. This document was prepared by the African delegation to the second meeting of the Africa-China-US Trilateral Dialogue, Beijing, 5-6 March 2007. The delegation comprised: Dr William Lyakurwa, Hon. Sydney Mufamadi, Hon. Patrick Mazimhaka, Michael Spicer, Amb. Joe Mollo, Hon. Lopo do Nascimento, and Dr Greg Mills. Please note that the views expressed remain those of the individuals alone, and should not be taken to reflect any official position. © The Brenthurst Foundation/Do Nascimento, Lyakurwa, Mazimhaka, Mills, Mollo, Mufamadi and Spicer.

decolonization and nation-building, and the ideological struggle between capitalism and socialism. The next fifty years will be different. Today there is little disagreement in Africa about the importance of governance, the principles of economic organization and management, and commitment to democratization. African governments have acknowledged the importance of economic and political interdependence and agreed on the mechanisms for achieving these goals: the constitutive act of the African Union and the New Partnership for Africa's Development.

Now that the Cold War is over, Africa does not have to pick sides. Partnerships should be based on an identification of Africa's own needs. Business competition is good for the continent; indeed, it can reduce costs for African consumers and increase revenues for its governments. And neither is competition a zero-sum game, occurring at the expense of one economy or the other.

African development goals are underpinned by a number of strategic tenets: access to technology and global markets, creation and maintenance of social peace, the establishment of environmental standards, transparent bidding and institutions, promotion of governance and sound economic management, transparency in aid giving, the maximization of revenues for African governments and electorates, and maximizing the effect of local conflict resolution and peacekeeping.

Africa's development path is likely to be differentiated according to the performance, governance and comparative advantages of its nations. Given China's industrial pre-eminence, African development is unlikely to come from high-volume manufacturing. Asian countries will probably dominate industries like cheap clothing or footwear for a generation or more, thereby inhibiting most African countries from climbing the traditional first step of the industrialization ladder. A combination of natural resource exploitation, agricultural self-sufficiency and high-value agro-exports, and the expansion of its unique range of service industries including tourism, would seem to be the most likely and rewarding growth path for many African states. China illustrates not only what is possible by managing an agricultural revolution, but how public and private initiatives can be productively integrated and managed.

This cannot simply be growth at all costs. Environmental factors and questions of social justice and the creation of a peaceful society along with democracy and human rights are all important.

For Africa, the critical issue in its relations with China and the US is the strengthening of governance institutions and the promotion of trade and investment links. External assistance needs to be aligned to clearly defined and articulated African needs. Africa is much more than a destination for increased aid or a source of energy and natural resources. It is not just a 'problem' to be 'solved'. It is rather a voice to be heard, and a partner of choice for the long term, beyond access to natural resources.

China's interest in Africa

The popular view from Africa, however, is that China's continental interest is mostly about trade and aid. At the China–Africa summit held in Beijing in November 2006, President Hu offered $5 billion in loans and credit to Africa along with a doubling of aid. During his February 2007 visit to Africa, Beijing also announced that it would lend African nations $3 billion in preferential credit over three years and double aid and interest-free loans at the same time. In 2006, trade between China and Africa reached $55.5 billion, a 40 per cent jump over 2005. Direct Chinese investment in Africa is now $6.6 billion, according to official Chinese sources.

But the figures do not tell the full story. The importance of China to Africa has to be understood in terms of China's own development path. Its real economic growth, which has averaged a shade under 9 per cent annually for the past thirty years, has been driven by year-on-year export growth averaging over 17 per cent. Export growth in 2006 alone exceeded 30 per cent. In 1980, China's share of world trade was less than 1 per cent; by 2003 it had risen to 6 per cent. This trade largely involves processing and assembly of components that come from elsewhere. China's shortage of minerals, energy, arable land and even water is as impressive as its abundance of labour and manufacturing capacity.

This helps to partly explain China's renewed interest in Africa. Chinese-led demand is driving up the prices and availability of the raw materials it needs. As the growth in the value of its exports inevitably slows as foreign and domestic markets saturate, China will need to continue expanding its economy and cater for its 1.4 billion expectant citizens by adding more Chinese 'content' to the same exports. To do that it needs to acquire and secure sources of raw materials.

Points of intersection: a coincidence of interests?

African countries face a conundrum with regard to China's changing relationship with the continent. African domestic industries, in textiles and other areas, are being swamped by cheaper Chinese products. Such concerns are raised by the investment trends of China (and the US) in Africa, which have tended to be in the oil sector which traditionally has not benefited African citizens for a range of reasons, including the nature of governance in those countries and macro-economic effects including the overvaluation of currencies. Oil booms have generally enriched Africa's elites, not its people, and have contributed to the plague of corruption in Africa – which is estimated today to cost the continent $150 billion annually. Like crime, corruption imposes a significant tax on development.

With only half of its energy needs now supplied by domestic sources, China has aggressively pursued oil interests in Africa, notably in the Sudan, which supplies one-tenth of all Chinese oil imports. Africa is more important as a share of China's oil supply than it is to the USA's, with Africa today supplying 25 per cent of China's oil and 15 per cent of the United States'.

The benefit Africa generates from such investment depends on what Africans do for themselves more than what China and the US can do for Africa. Good governance is a prerequisite for the higher-order investments in Africa that Africans consider essential, such as beneficiation of natural resources. It is of course crucial that Chinese and American economic activities not implicitly undermine good governance. One of the best guarantees that a venture will promote African interests is the length of its engagement: a company that builds factories and mine shafts has a greater stake in stability and responsible government than does the short-term speculator.

In addition, low human capacity, poor infrastructure and Africa's small market size (about the same size as the US state of Ohio) reduces its attractiveness to foreign investors. But more importantly, such investors follow the lead of their local African counterparts. The fact that Africans themselves are seen as significant divestors in their own countries (around 40 per cent of African capital has fled the continent) gives foreign investors scant confidence.

Contrary to the widespread perception that there is a contradiction between China's activities in Africa and improved standards of African governance and democracy, good governance is actually in China's long-term interest because it is the best way to ensure that investor interests are safeguarded – a realization that Western countries have long since arrived at in Africa. Similarly democracies have consistently performed better economically than autocracies (outside of East Asia about 50 per cent faster growth between 1960–2003), hence promotion of democracy is also in the investor's enlightened self-interest. Moreover, support for autocratic governments by external powers is likely to pit them against African citizens who had consistently fought for such rights.

There are other areas where external powers share interests with Africa. Support for African peacemaking efforts goes beyond technical support. It has to be undergirded by political consensus and co-ordination, without which such efforts run the risk of incoherence and costly failure. The absence of unity of international effort runs the risk of the infection of entire regions – viz. Sudan and Darfur. Africa can ill afford to be used as a bargaining chip in any political contest.

The trajectory of African democracy suggests that internal developments are no longer a strictly sovereign affair. Africa has today replaced 'non-interference' in domestic affairs with the principle of 'non-indifference'. All this is in line with the contemporary movement towards human and not simply state-centric security, and with the lesson that civil wars do not fix themselves. Chinese and American support in the United Nations for fully funded African peacekeeping missions would not only be practically expedient but a signal of political partnership, as would their co-operation over painfully intractable issues such as Darfur. Even so, bilateral actions must be viewed as part of overarching multilateral agreements towards the goal of sustainable security and development.

A 'win–win' strategy?

Care must thus be taken not to view Africa exclusively through the optic of foreign energy security. Instead, cognisance has to be taken of Africa's own strategic development and security needs.

Can the interests of China, the US and Africa be reconciled? Potentially but not automatically. 'Yes' – if Africa can strike beneficiation and exploration partnerships, and if China and the US seek to improve governance standards. Even though China and the US are acting in their own self-interest in deepening their ties with Africa in the resources sector, Africa should not be afraid of losing out. Lasting relationships need to be mutually beneficial.

Efforts to establish control of supplies of raw materials will be both a challenge and an opportunity for those African nations intent on adding more value domestically to their commodities through increased local beneficiation.

The impact of China's increased aid to Africa on the dominant Western aid paradigm in Africa must be viewed in this light. This paradigm today can be explained in terms of the promotion of governance and democracy rather than simply the securing of narrow national interests. Overall, aid has to be offered in a manner that strengthens African institutions, encourages transparency, improves macro-economic policies, develops national and regional infrastructure, assists technical capacity-building, and facilitates the growth of Africa's productive sector, notably in agriculture and manufacturing. Aid-giving must align with African needs – promoting growth and enhancing continental

productive capacity. The facilitation of foreign direct investment flows and assistance in improving credit risk ratings are
similarly in the long-term African interest. Ultimately, however,
as with East Asia, development will demand investment rather
than solely aid-based strategies. Development will depend more
on how aid is used by Africans than on how much is given by
outsiders. Any worthwhile 'development dialogue' with Africa
has to encompass the creation of a local enabling environment
to compete for investment.

From the above a number of possible trilateral Africa–China–
US governance mechanisms emerge.

It may be necessary to create a new set of principles on how
business should be done with Africa. Such principles could
include the importance of giving African people democratic
choice, as well as issues of mutual interest around conflict pre-
vention, integration into the world economy, health care, energy,
good governance, and capacity building. Africans must write
and own these principles if they are to succeed in the twenty-
first century.

What the burgeoning Chinese and American interests in
Africa show is overwhelmingly positive: It moves the prevailing
view of Africa from a mindset where engagement is driven by aid
and humanitarian instinct to one of partnership and commercial
opportunity. It is motivated not by a spirit of benevolence but
one of mutual opportunity. In so doing, it shows Africa has an
increasing stake in the global economy.

8

And what about India and Africa? The road ahead

SUMIT ROY

The chapters in this book explore different views of the relation-ship between China and Africa. This is all very well, but India, too, along with China, is a rising power in a globalizing world and has been forging strong ties with Africa. In this respect, my approach empathizes with the thoughts espoused by Stephen Chan in his all-embracing essay on misconceptions and false illusions about the China–Africa relationship. The core message of this chapter is that the growing exchange over trade and in-vestment between India and Africa has been galvanized by a shift in diplomatic strategy from politics to economics. This impinges on African structural change and development and invades the territory of politics and culture. The interaction should be seen as a facet of Africa's complex interplay with nations and institu-tions within and beyond the continent. Ultimately, however, African nations, and above all people, have to harness their inner strengths to pursue their own vision of development.

The India–Africa ties emerge in the frame of globalization – a historical process – which is the major challenge in the twenty-first century. It encapsulates compression, a 'blurring of borders', interlocking of nations, and mounting transnational relations. In this realm China and India are seen as the 'emerging giants' which are reshaping the world economy. This encompasses the intensification of their links with developing regions. Though China has been the focus of analysts, India, too, has been growing fast at about 8.2 per cent over 2006-11 (compound annual growth rate). But poverty, low per capita income, and inequality are major challenges. The India–Africa links are underscored by notions of 'mutual support', 'reciprocity' and 'interdependence'.

However, Africa has to evolve forceful economic and political policies within and beyond the region to pursue its own vision. This has to be underscored by 'good governance' – a concept encapsulating democracy, basic needs and basic rights. The economy has been driven by trade. Its share of world trade has been declining – about 3 per cent (2006) compared with that of Asia, whose share has doubled to 27.6 per cent (2006). Growth in Africa was limited over the period 1980-2000, with an average annual growth rate of only 1.1 per cent. However, it has been rising in recent years, albeit in a fluctuating manner: 5.7 per cent (2006), 5.3 per cent (2005), and 5.2 per cent (2004), with marked regional variations. The rate in 2006 was below that of developing Asia, at 8.7 per cent, and the Millennium Development Goals target of 7 per cent to curb poverty. Africa has to embrace globalization, which can usher in economies of scale, access to wider markets, and a shift from raw materials to processed and manufactured goods. In the long run, an international market, coupled with the use of cheaper imported inputs, could enable industry to be more competitive. This could create jobs through labour-intensive production. FDI, too, has to be mobilized to attract investment in the core sectors, alongside resource-based ones – infrastructure (physical and human), services and newer industries with export potential. Links through trade and FDI have to be promoted. Aid, though declining, has also been supportive, and especially for those with heavy external debts. Overcoming economic obstacles has to be accompanied by measures to reduce the inter- and intra-state conflicts and tensions which bedevil the continent.

India has often cited its long historical relationship with Africa. Indeed, this can be traced to the precolonial period. This was firmly rooted in migration and commerce in the eighteenth century. Indeed, trade and other economic relations between India and Africa existed long before colonialism. The Indian connection of business contacts with East Africa was utilized by traders – imports, exports and shipping. Mahatma Gandhi's satyagraha movement in South Africa (1906–1914) fought for the rights of Indians. Gandhi firmly emphasized that the relationship between India and Africa should not be based on conventional trade and exploitation, as in the colonial period, but on human exchange:

> the commerce between India and Africa will be of ideas and services, not of manufactured goods against raw materials after the fashion of western exploiters.[1]

Gandhi's vision may be idealistic but it poses ideas for reflection on the future of India–Africa ties.

In the post-Cold War era thinking in India on Africa was based on five mantras: economic cooperation, engaging the PIOs (Persons of Indian Origin), preventing and combating terrorism, preserving peace, and assisting the African defence forces. After independence (1947) Jawaharlal Nehru, the Indian prime

---

1. In R. Beri, 'India's Africa Policy in the Post Cold War Era', *Strategic Analysis*, April-June 2003, pp. 222-3.

minister, laid the foundation of India's policy on Africa. This was centred on two fronts: first, the struggle against colonization and racial discrimination in South Africa; second, on Persons of Indian Origin. Few African nations supported India on the diplomatic front in multilateral forums such as the Non-Aligned Movement. However, in the mid-1960s India reassessed its Africa links and pursued fresh initiatives. Economic diplomacy with Africa improved in the 1970s in the context of more emphasis on South–South cooperation, evidenced in the Lagos Plan of Action (1980). Over the past four decades India has provided more than US$2 billion in technical assistance to countries in the South. The bulk of this went to Africa. In the last decade a number of initiatives promoted trade with the African private sector. Most of the Indian imports from Africa were resource-based products, while Indian exports to Africa consisted of textiles, pharmaceuticals and engineering products.

The exchange between Asia (encompassing India and China and smaller nations in the region) and Africa has been growing fast since 2000. The trend is positive. But Africa's growth of exports still remains relatively small from the Asian angle. However, Asia's exports to Africa are growing rapidly (18 per cent per annum). At the same time, the composition of Africa's exports to Asia is biased towards primary and resource-based goods (especially energy), while that of Asia to Africa comprises manufactured and consumer goods. This has boosted African commodity export income in the short term. But in the medium to long term it is essential that they diversify their exports – shift from agriculture to services, industry and technology. Alongside this, it is essential for Asian countries such as India to curb high mutual tariffs, non-tariff barriers and tariff escalation to stimulate African exports. Foreign direct investment, too, over the last decade has been capital-intensive and based on extractive industries and linkages, with the rest of the economy having been left weak. The impact on employment creation and poverty reduction has been limited. Gradually, however, investment in other sectors is increasing: infrastructure, apparel, agro-processing, power generation, road construction, tourism and telecommunications. This has the potential of transferring appropriate technology from major Asian countries, such as India, to Africa and easing the latter's entry into the global value chain.

India's major recent trade and investment links are with countries such as South Africa and Nigeria, but it is endeavouring to embrace smaller nations in Africa. Its ongoing inroads into the continent are claimed to be driven by the 'quest for resources, business opportunities, diplomatic initiatives and strategic partnerships'. Oil and gas are understandably crucial to meet its rising energy inputs for industrialization. It imports about 75 per cent of its oil. This could rise to 90 per cent over the next decade. The Indian state-owned Oil and Natural Gas Company (ONGC) has secured exploration contracts and related energy projects in Africa through its international division ONGC Videsh Ltd (OVL) in various countries including Nigeria and Sudan. In 2005 OVL entered into a joint venture with LN Mittal Steel (renamed Arcelor Mittal) – the world's largest multinational steel corporation – to form ONGC Mittal Energy Ltd, which negotiated a contract worth US$6 billion for infrastructure with Nigeria. This was in exchange for two offshore oil exploration rights. OVL has undertaken similar projects in Ivory Coast, Libya, Egypt and Gabon. However, in terms of oil deals, India has been outsmarted by China.

Indian companies have been moving into sectors such as copper mining investment (Zambia), iron ore and steel refining (Liberia and Nigeria). They have invested in infrastructure.

Rites and Ircon, for instance, state-owned infrastructure and engineering companies, have supported Africa's rail and road development and engineering companies. Recent investment patterns in Africa illuminate future possibilities: a range of manufactures, chemicals and pharmaceuticals, iron and steel, textiles, mining, infrastructure, transport, banking and retail. Trade usually follows such flows. This impacts in different ways on African economies. India's role as an investor and as a source of civil and other engineering countries has been intensified by major private companies (the Tata Group, Mittal Steel) and public ones (Rites, Ircon). This has been supported by the Indian state through credit (e.g. Exim) to boost India's export drive in key sectors (e.g. agriculture, power, transport, manufacturing and IT). Indeed, lines of credit amounting to some $1.5 billion have funded projects in agriculture, transport, power, and manufacturing and capacity building. India has also set up a pan-African e-network (IT). This links fifty-three African countries to Indian universities and hospitals to facilitate the development of critical human capital – health and education.

The interaction between India and Africa has been galvanized by a shift in strategy from politics to economic development – from support for nationalist movements to combat colonization to infrastructure and economic development. This is encapsulated in diplomatic dialogues, meetings, visits and summits to assess the resources required to stimulate growth in and through the core sectors. This set targets on trade, investment and aid. Pledges and promises have driven the urge to forge closer ties, notwithstanding sometimes sharp contrasts between the rhetoric and the practice.

The partnership between India and Africa is promising, though only time will show whether the exchange is balanced and mutual. Much depends on the bargaining capacity of African leaders vis-à-vis the Indian state and its representatives. This is exemplified by the India-Africa Delhi Summit of 2008, which followed the China-Africa Beijing Summit of 2006. The Indian summit centred on trade, energy and cooperation on global issues such as UN reform, terrorism and climate change. The Delhi Declaration and the Framework for Cooperation emerged; the first was a political document covering bilateral, regional and international issues of Indian and Africa interest (UN reform, WTO, terrorism); the second covered areas of cooperation, including education, science and technology, agricultural productivity, food security, industrial growth, infrastructure and health. Pledges were made to double India–Africa trade to $50 billion by 2012. This should be seen against a backdrop of rising bilateral trade between India and Africa between 1991 and 2006/7.

The pledge to support African development was reaffirmed at the Second India-Africa Forum Summit in Addis Ababa, Ethiopia, in May 2011. The aim to boost trade from $45 billion in 2011 to $70 billion by 2015, and provide aid of $500 million in addition to the $5.4 billion already promised, was emphasized. In addition there were plans to enhance capacity-building through the setting up of regional centres of excellence, training centres, and skill training in different African countries over the next five years. There was also discussion on curbing piracy and terrorism and mutually supporting the goal of an Indian and an African seat on the UN Security Council. However, India is still behind China in terms of building its links with Africa. India's trade with Africa in 2010 was estimated to be $45 billion, in contrast to China's $130 billion. Though the financial crisis (2008) initially adversely affected India and China, both nations promised to go on building their economic ties with Africa. Moreover, BRICS (Brazil, Russia, India, China and South Africa) could induce radical change of the Bretton Woods institutions (IMF, World Bank, WTO) and the UN to establish more equitable exchange over global finance, trade and investment. This could enhance the prospects of development and peace in Africa.

Controversies, however, have surfaced over the nature of investments by India in Africa – exemplified by its deals with Sudan over oil exploration and trade agreements with Zimbabwe, which has been a target of sanctions by developed nations. There have also been questions over the renting of land in African countries by India to produce food and other crops for re-export. This impinges on sensitive issues of land acquisition, displacement and resettlement of peasants, and the role of states in the respective countries. At the same time, India's role in peacekeeping could ease inter- and intra-state conflicts in Africa.

Structural change in Africa through ties with 'rising powers' such as India presents obstacles in the short term. But in the medium to long term the exchange, if properly managed by African nations, could enhance their development. This requires assessing the scope of diversification, alongside regular monitoring and evaluation of such relationships in different African countries. In this respect, useful insights can be gleaned from India's experiments with development. Indeed, both could share their experiences. In contrast to China, India offers a 'mixed' economy model with a 'thriving democracy' and political diversity. Moreover, despite its recent high growth rate India shares many features with Africa: low levels of 'human development', poverty, income inequality, high levels of illiteracy, poor health, and struggles to improve the status of women, aside from political tensions. Indeed, some of these indicators are worse in India than in some African countries (e.g. Botswana). Like Africa, India also has to cope with obstacles due to inter- and intra-state conflicts – border clashes, demands for autonomy by states, intensification of internal terrorism, and frictions due to intense poverty and rural–urban and inter-group inequalities. At the same time, India's use of development strategies is relevant to African structural transformation – the 'Green Revolution' (1960s) to boost food security, IT to usher in technological and structural change, and democratic politics to cope with internal strife. The role of the state and the market, too, furnishes useful notions of interaction between the two forces in formulating policies on liberalization. The Indian government has also stated that its policies should not undermine African development. The support of Indian companies to implement measures to help Africa build a manufacturing base and enable it to supply intermediate and raw materials to India's export-oriented factories and the domestic economy offers hope. Such policies help occasion structural change in Africa.

Essentially, African countries have to devise forceful responses in their exchange with India to enable them to confront the major new challenges stemming from globalization. This unfolds in the context of their ties with regions and institutions within and beyond Africa, underscored by the pursuit of 'good governance'. The India–Africa exchange should be seen simply as one facet, albeit an important one, of a dynamic phase, which African states and their people have to harness and wield. Herein may lie a possible way of revitalizing the economy, culture and history of the so-called 'dark' continent which has dazzled, mystified and confused many nations. It has to shape and execute strategies through key institutions at local (including civil and social movements), national and international levels. Its policymakers have to juggle their bargaining strategies vis-à-vis India and other rising powers and developed nations. This could enable Africa to integrate meaningfully into a changing world.

AFTERWORD

The future of China and Africa

STEPHEN CHAN

China has gone through many phases in Africa. Patrick Mazimhaka points up the exploratory contacts in medieval times, and counterposes these with the more brutal Portuguese varieties. However, the contemporary age has already seen three distinct phases of Chinese involvement – with a fourth just beginning.

First was the phase of Bandung and what came after the Conference of 1955. It was a phase of genuine idealism accompanying what became non-alignment, and the beginnings of munificence towards Africa.

Second was the Cold War phase, in which approaches to Africa were conditioned, at least partly and sometimes seriously, in terms of competition not so much with the West but with the Soviet Union. Amid the contradictions that arose, China was monetheless deeply involved in the success of more than one liberation movement.

Third was the recent phase – the one that has caused a type of panic in the West – involving front-loaded Chinese aid, lines of liquidity and massive civil engineering provision, in exchange for long-term access to mineral and oil extraction, even at the risk of identified deposits being 'upstream' or without assured developed access or conditions for such.

However, the fourth phase, which has now begun, is to do with the growth of Chinese diasporic populations in Africa. These have direct ties with China, but include a large number of private entrepreneurs not necessarily within the ambit of direct Chinese state or Party control. The different generations and classes of Chinese have produced communities that both stick together and manifest profound cleavages and fault lines. Criminality has been exported from mainland China into these communities, which has often been compounded by corrupt relationships with African officials. Issues of race, class, financial impropriety and corruption will be among those that attend this fourth phase. To date, little scholarly work has been done on the subject. Ph.D. research at the School of Oriental and African Studies by Cornelia Schiller on the competing migrant generations of the Chinese diaspora in Madagascar, including study of the elements of criminality and the degree of integration into local culture and society, is nearing completion.

Previous generations have seen marked and successful integration, or at least solidarity. At the 1955 Freedom Congress in Kliptown, Soweto, the huge number of South African opponents of apartheid were fed by Chinese grocers in the township. Fay Chung, the Zimbabwean nationalist and cabinet minister, both supported the war of liberation and served the post-independence government. Jean Ping, the immediate past chairman of the Commission of the African Union, was half-Chinese. However, more recent migrants have had to begin the process of integration anew – and they are finding a larger diaspora and thus a greater range of purely Chinese relationships. Being able to live within one's own community can often hinder integration into the host society, or even any deep understanding of that culture. Beijing cannot do anything about this. Yet it will cause difficulties in official China–Africa relations, and pose new social and racial problems for African countries.

Whether this might lead to the sorts of problems faced by Indian populations in certain countries – in Amin's Uganda, for instance – remains to be seen. The Indian experience has not been a uniform one. The Indian community in Lusaka hid Kenneth Kaunda when he was on the run from the British colonial authorities, and he began reading the works of Gandhi while in Indian care. The problems the Indian community faced in Uganda are certainly not comparable to those that were faced in Zambia. In South Africa, Indian members of the ANC played outstanding roles in the fight against apartheid, and a portrait of Gandhi sat alongside one of Marx in Govan Mbeki's house. Having said that, the fate of the Ugandan Indians represents a warning of what could happen to Chinese communities if they own too much, integrate too little and abuse their employees. Not that this can be said to be an accurate depiction of what happened in Uganda – but perception and the political use of perception become everything.

The world is coming to Africa. Or at least the world in coming in greater numbers and as a greater force to Africa. China and India have always been there in the modern era. But they have been there in different ways in different epochs. Each epoch introduces new possibilities and new vulnerabilities. The problem with much Western analysis of China in Africa is that it often takes what I call the third phase as something new and undermining of Western interests. The concern is not so much any undermining of African interests – that is added as a justifying afterthought – but of Western interests in the first instance. Yet

Chinese economic penetration of Africa is hardly a persistent and consistent rival of Western investment and trade volumes. In volume terms, the West still holds immense sway. It is hard to resist sometimes the arch observation that those who seek to dominate the postcolonial world still cannot bear to see the relationships of the colonial world unduly disrupted. In that sense, the West had simply better get used to China in Africa, and also to the surge in Indian presence there as well.

This also means there needs to be a process of catching up, in the scholarly literature, with a rapidly evolving and changing situation. There are now hopeful developments in this literature, and a witness to that is the detailing of relationships between China and specific African countries. I had mentioned earlier what many might view as surprising changes in the relationship between Angola and China, and books on this relationship have now begun to be published.[1] Some of the hopeful and speculative literature on both the South African[2] and Chinese sides[3] now seems dated, but the judicious overview of Chris Alden still seems prescient[4] and the detailed arguments of Deborah Brautigam still wise and cogent[5] - even if, in the United States, hers remains a minority voice amid the political angst about China, for its economic posture in the USA, never mind in Africa. What is needed is a monographic literature addressing what will likely be a key case example for the future: the relationship between China and Zambia, with its sometimes violent

---

1. Lucy Corkin, *Uncovering African Agency: Angola's Management of China's Credit Lines*, Farnham: Ashgate, 2013; Marcus Power and Ana Cristina Alves, eds, *China and Angola - A Marriage of Convenience?*, Cape Town: Pambazuka, 2012.

2. *China in Africa*, special issue of *South African Journal of International Affairs*, vol. 13, no. 1, 2006.

3. *The Symposium of China-Africa Shared Development*, Beijing: Chinese Academy of Social Sciences, 2006.

4. Chris Alden, *China in Africa*, London: Zed Books, 2007.

5. Deborah Brautigam, *The Dragon's Gift: The Real Story of China in Africa*, Oxford: Oxford University Press, 2009.

industrial disputes involving the deaths of both Zambian miners and Chinese managers. Such studies will also need to look into the era of private ownership of Zambian mines immediately before the recent Chinese purchase of many of them - that is, a brief period of Indian ownership, accompanied by asset-stripping and malpractice. Work will also be needed on the Democratic Republic of the Congo, where, notwithstanding Western watering down of Chinese ambitions, there is the question as to whether the huge Chinese investment in southern DRC can be sustained and bring benefits to a beleaguered population, as well as to the unavoidable and unavoidably avaricious political figures of the region.

In this context, what will also be needed in the future are a number of localized trilateral dialogues - leading to a species of what the International Labour Organization has called 'tripartite agreements', in which governments, managements and unions are all involved in mapping out sustainable regimes of cooperation, consultation, continuing representation, fairness and safety.

I have tried in this book to indicate, however, that - from the Chinese perspective - there has been established a positive foundation for the way China and Africa might approach the future. The collection has sought to provide an antidote to the sense that this is just another era of exploitation. This is not to say there is no exploitation. It is to say that, just as the West expands and conducts its relationships on its terms and within its 'values' - which are broadcast as moral and righteous - so too do the Chinese. In that sense, it has been a simple book. That is, it would have said something simple had not many long years of antagonism, rivalry, competition and prejudice not made a simple statement a hazardous one - and assuredly, in the responses to come, it will be described as an immoral work. The book has simply sought to say that the Chinese government may be discerned and has understood itself – notwithstanding debate, reflected in this book – to have operated a moral economy within Africa. Many in Africa feel this has been the case.

There are also those in Africa who feel that Africa is mature enough to deal equitably and on equal terms with China – and with America too.

Contributors

JERRY C.Y. LIU is Professor at the National Taiwan University of the Arts.

QING CAO is Senior Lecturer at the University of Durham in the United Kingdom.

L.H.M. LING is Associate Professor at the New School in New York.

XIAOMING HUANG is Professor at the Victoria University of Wellington in New Zealand.

PATRICK MAZIMHAKA was Deputy Chairman of the Council of the African Union, and was a member of the Trilateral Dialogue on China, Africa and the United States.

SUMIT ROY is Visiting Senior Research Fellow at Jadavpur University in Kolkata, India.

Index

INDEX 149

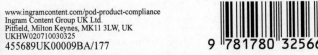